The Wonder Within You

From the Metaphysical Journals of
David Manners

By David Manners

Edited and with an introduction by
David Morgan Jones

Wise Child Press

Also by David Manners:

Nonfiction
Look Through: An Evidence of SELF Discovery
Awakening from the Dream of Me

Fiction
Convenient Season
Under Running Laughter

Cover painting and design: A view of David Manners' house at Yucca Loma ranch by Jan Kiker.

The Wonder Within You

By David Manners

Contents

Acknowledgements

Many wonderful people participated in the journey of fulfilling David Manners' wish of producing a book from his metaphysical journals. I benefited in so many ways from their support and encouragement during this project.

Foremost, thank you to Mrs. Rachel Samuel (Levey) in Birmingham, Alabama. You trusted me with the original materials David entrusted to you, which was just one of your many amazing gifts to me. Your belief that I could not only do this project but also do it the way David would want encouraged me whenever I felt lost. Thank you for sharing so openly your memories of David. And now I have the honor of wonderful memories of your friendship.

To Sandy Jones in Ojai, California: Without you, this project likely would not have started. Your choice of answering an e-mail from a stranger and then your trust in introducing me to Rachel Samuel changed the direction of my life for the next three years. Sandy is the force behind **www.williamsamuel.com**. I encourage readers to visit this Web site to learn more about his ideas and his work.

To John Bailey in St. Paul, Minnesota: John edited and published David's book Awakening from the Dream of Me. John, thank you for your encouragement and copies of the book, and thank you for your generosity in approving use of material from Awakening.

To Rick McKay in New York City: Rick conducted and wrote the last interviews David gave before his death. Thank you, Rick, for your notes of encouragement and for meeting with me during your promotion schedule for your documentary *Broadway: The Golden Age*. Readers can learn more about Rick's important multi-award-winning film at **www.rickmckay.com**.

To John Norris in Nashville, Tennessee: John, who knew David for many years, created the Web site **www.davidmanners.com**. This wonderfully complete and beautifully designed site is a delight for film fans and anyone who wants to know more about David and his Hollywood career. John, thank you for our discussions about David. May they continue.

I benefited from wonderful reviews of the introduction. To Dr. Domino Perez, of the University of Texas at Austin, thank you for your academic, film, writing, and editing expertise. To Mollie McNair, editor extraordinaire, in Atlanta, Georgia, thank you for your insights and discussion. And to my sister (and friend) Beth Jones in Covington, Kentucky, thank you for your unconditional support, which means so much to me.

To Jan Kiker in Austin, Texas: Thank you for the beautiful cover and for your eagerness to contribute to this project.

And finally to David Manners, wherever you are. I talked so much to your photo on my desk that I feel we have met. I hope your spirit approves of this book.

David Morgan Jones

Text note: David Manners used the terms *man, mankind,* and *he* to refer all people. The terms are not meant to exclude anyone.

Part 1

Biographical introduction

> I am not a preacher, a writer, or a teacher. I am only one man who loves God above all else and would serve God in all my ways.
>
> David Manners, Journal 5, 16 Nov 1979

A journey toward wonder

Antiques and art dealer . . . forester . . . outdoorsman . . . Broadway actor . . . Hollywood star . . . guest-ranch owner . . . best-selling novelist . . . artist . . . metaphysician and philosopher . . .

These roles identify the interests and occupations of David Manners, but they offer no insight into his life-long spiritual quest. David disliked labels because he saw them as dualistic. Although he assumed all these roles at different times in his life (1900 to 1998), he would have resisted acknowledging them as emphasizing outer appearance and ego and as not recognizing the inner world of Spirit, which is our true essence as human beings.

David Manners and his quest for understanding God and for living in Truth is the focus of *The Wonder Within You*. Except for this introduction, all text comes from the 27 journals that David kept from 1978 to 1993 and from newsletters he published from about the same time. David came to view these journals as "a conversation between the soul and the Spirit." (Journal 8, 9 Oct 1982)

This introduction is not a biography of David Manners—that is for another book at another time. It is not an analysis of his film career or a critique of his novels. It is intended as context for knowing about the spirituality of the man and for contemplating his words of immense power and understanding. The sections that follow in this introduction interweave David's journey toward wonder, as he wrote about them in his journals, with the related events of his life.

Conversation between the soul and the Spirit

David began his quest for enlightenment as a young child. His search grew in intensity through his young adult years, until it became the central focus of his life at the height of his success in Hollywood in the 1930s. This focus contributed greatly to his leaving Hollywood permanently in 1936 and settling in the Mojave Desert to concentrate on discarding the influences of past training and the religions of others to search for his own understanding.

David had already studied the tenets of the Anglican Church (the church of his parents), Episcopal Church, and the Roman Catholic Church. These were followed by an investigation of Theosophy, especially when he befriended Jiddu Krishnamurti for a time between 1919 and the early 1930s, before and after Krishnamurti split with the Theosophists to begin his own path as a spiritual leader.

During David's time in the desert, he studied Christian Science, Unity School of Christianity, and Religious Science, Zen, and Buddhism. David read the works of Emerson, Mary Baker Eddy, Joel Goldsmith, Charles and Myrtle Fillmore, Ernest Holmes,

Marie Watts, H. B. Jeffrey, and William Samuel—all in the New Thought mode. He read the works of Rumi, the 13th century Persian mystic; he studied Zen, the teachings of the Buddha, and the teachings of Lao-tzu. He studied the New Testament for insights into the messages of Jesus.

In 1984, after years of religious and philosophic study, he wrote that the books that most influenced his understanding were *The Teaching of Huang Po, The Gospel According to Thomas,* the gospels of Matthew and John, *The Mustard Seed* (by Rajneesh), *The Art of Meditation, and The Art of Spiritual Healing* (both by Goldsmith). (Journals 10 and 11, 18 Feb and 11 Apr 1984)

When he was ready to distill his ideas from this quest, he published two books of his own metaphysical concepts: *Look Through: An Evidence of SELF Discovery* (The Seed Center, Palo Alto, CA, 1971, reprinted 1978) and *Awakening from the Dream of Me* (Non-Stop Books, Minneapolis, MN, 1987), both now out of print. He worked on other books that he eventually discarded in favor of keeping his journals (he continued to work on novels, too, which he also destroyed).

During his years of journaling, David also published a quarterly newsletter that he continued into his 90s, and he occasionally submitted short pieces to metaphysical and philosophical magazines. Through the 1980s, he recorded tapes for a small but growing distribution list.

The Wonder Within You represents the maturity of his thinking after *Look Through* and *Awakening* were published and shows the further influence of his great friend and fellow metaphysician William Samuel (Levey). In fact, William wrote the introductions to both of David's metaphysical books. David met William Samuel in 1969 at one of his lectures in California and immediately resonated with William's ideas. David recognized their practicality and clarity.

Such concepts of William's as our original nature as the child within and the principle of transcendent awareness and identity were published in *A Guide to Awareness and Tranquility* (1967), *Two Plus Two Equals Reality* (1969), and *The Child Within Us Lives!* (1986) Samuel's writings and teachings synthesize science, religion, and metaphysics into a clear explanation of enlightenment.

These ideas resounded with truth for David, and he continued close contact with William and his wife Rachel Samuel through visits and almost daily letter writing until William's death in 1996, after which David continued his close friendship with Rachel, a metaphysician in her own right. It is to her as literary executor that David entrusted his journals for eventual editing and publication after his death.

The soundless voice

> God speaks a silent tongue in my heart and is the reality I am. There is no other. I feel it. All else is of no real substance.
>
> Journal 9, 20 Mar 1983

David sat in silence everyday listening for the inner voice that he believed to be Spirit directing him and filling him with joy and understanding. With a notepad on his knee or at a table or desk—wherever he happened to be—David wrote the words he felt directed to write. He included ideas from his years of study that he felt resonated Truth. All the while, David's goal was to shine a light that would help others find their way for themselves.

As long as there are words in mind and a pen and paper, I shall go on trying to make others understand, and if one is helped to walk out from the shadow into Light, what more can I ask?

Journal 10, 28 Jan 1984

The upshot of all these words, lectures, the books, the tapes is to present reality here and now, the availability of heaven.

Journal 5, 23 Dec 1979

David did not intend to create a dogma or a group of believers around him or his perceived personality. He believed that, "There is no word, no person who can open the doors of heaven for us. Only we can do that, and it is not done through any system or organization." (Journal 11, 3 Jul 1984) He intended his journals to be free of reticence by boldly stating his truth:

Tell it as it is—free of all attempts to please, to conform, or to hope for a reader. Let it be!

Journal 1, 19 May 1978

He pursued the concepts of Is-ness and I AM as ways to understand conscious awareness, which is that inner knowing, free of personal judgment that connects one with Spirit. He understood Is-ness as the unadulterated awareness of God as omnipresent; he understood I AM as the love and energy radiance of God. Further, he believed I AM to be the only reality and that understanding this is "to be at peace and to experience the joy, wonder, and delight of ineffable Love." (Journal 4, 19 May 1979)

David's great accomplishment in his journals and newsletters is his ability to describe complex concepts in simple, accessible language. Readers can judge this for themselves in the other sections of this book, but the following is one example in which David discusses his understanding and does not allow terms to block seeing truth:

> God expresses in infinite form, color, and modes of communication. All have their place and purpose. Never feel thwarted by a term that says nothing to you because of your conditioning. Terms are as individual as you are, as the I AM is. Does the term speak to your I AM? If not discard it, or better still, find your own term.
>
> Journal 2, 21 Sept 1978

The David Manners who faithfully recorded these thoughts in his journals led as interesting a life as the roles that began this essay would indicate. In David's own words, whenever possible, the next sections examine the background that produced his beliefs.

Forces of influence

Rauff de Ryther Daun Aklom was born to George Moreby Acklom and Lilian Manners on 30 April 1900 in Halifax, Nova Scotia. He was the couple's second child, following Dorothea Cecily Acklom, born in 1898. Lilian, born in England, and George, born in India to a British civil servant, were both descendants of historic, noble British families. David's lengthy name paid homage to surnames in the Acklom family tree. He once remarked to William Samuel, "Do you wonder that I changed it?" (letter, 5 Feb 1986)

Lilian, a concert pianist, was a direct descendant of William the Conqueror, and her family seat was Belvoir Castle and Haddon Hall, homes of the Duke of Rutland. George, a descendant of the family that gave its name to the village of Acklam (a variant spelling) in Yorkshire, England, was educated at Queen's College, Cambridge, graduating with an M.A. in 1894.

George was a man of many interests, whose career included being a professor of English, of Mathematics, master of a prestigious boy's school, and ultimately, a 40-year career as editor at E. P. Dutton in New York City.

In 1907, George moved the family from Halifax to New York City to join Dutton. The family, comfortably well off in monetary terms, was not rich in warmth.

> I find digging back is depressing. No laughter, no love. I passed my mother and was afraid of the father. I was dour, stolid. I see no happy child. Sturdy, yes, and stolid. The word seems to be gloomy. I honestly don't want to look back. It is not happy. Youth and childhood were not happy. I am lighter and happier now than as a child.
>
> Journal 18, 13 Dec 1986

The Acklom household was disrupted as a battle of wills between father and son ensued. David was often beaten to the point of bleeding. Cecily played the part of big-sister protector, when she and David weren't producing plays together for visitors. Lilian favored her son in battles with his father, so David believed his father was jealous of Lilian's and Cecily's closeness to him.

> I recall being at the top of the stairs when I saw Lilian, who had been away, and I was so happy to see her again. I began to rush down to her arms, but George stepped between us. He was holding a riding whip, which he flicked back and forth across the stairway. I ran on, and I got the whip across my face. I grabbed George's leg and bit hard.

He yelped and stepped aside, and I was in Lilian's arms. I wonder if George ever forgave me. He whipped me often, unmercifully, but to the end of her life, Lilian was my best friend.

Journal 18, 27 Oct 1986

David characterized his early childhood as having, ". . .a 'mummy' but no 'daddy.' Daddy was distant, cross, criticizing, and I was afraid of him. I heard him caning boys at school, and I heard their cries and the angry slashes of the stick. I was afraid of him. I had no father to love." (Journal 17, 5 Nov 1986)

The differences between father and son became competitive in other ways when David grew older. George was an expert chess player, and he was determined to teach the game to David. "The kid pouted and played dumb and made the old man rave to Lilian that they had a moron for a son. George gave up and that was okay with the kid. . . ." (Letter to William Samuel, 6 July 1986)

David was not the exceptional student that his parents were—his nickname in high school was "slow freight"—and the constant berating by his father only supported David's feeling that he was inferior. This feeling of inferiority influenced David's opinion of himself throughout his life, often referring to himself as slow or dimwitted.

> When I was a child of 10 or 11, I was often accused by the parent of being "empty headed." I know I was not because I was full of dreams and not intellectually proficient. If I had really been empty, it wouldn't have taken a lifetime to see Truth.
>
> Journal 9, 20 Mar 1983

Successfully publishing novels and his metaphysical books didn't change his opinion of himself. However, he used the characteristic to guide his search for truth:

> I am not a big brain, and I cannot read the big brains without being slightly sick or feeling like I am drowning in water in which I can't swim. It takes a lot of stillness to get back. I wonder if stillness is an anathema to the big brains. The simplest, most childlike approach is the road for this one. Maybe it is for many others who do not know it and who look for it in the complications of modern living (Western) where I can't see it.
>
> Journal 10, 1 Jan 1984

Belief and doubt

> When I was a young man, it was emotion: the more emotional, the more spiritual, I believed. Now, there is no emotion at all. It is beyond emotion. It is a pulsing energy that is expressed as stillness.
>
> Journal 6, 22 Dec 1981

As a teenager, David channeled his energy into the Episcopal Church and into writing and acting. He immersed himself in church activities, including singing in the choir and serving as an altar boy, even working as a counselor at summer camps and retreats sponsored by his diocese. He reveled in the praise he received from others, noting in a letter to Rachel Samuel that one matron had said, "'Oh, that boy is so devout!' The ego really liked to hear things like that." (7 Jan 1986)

David saw his early connection to the Episcopal Church as the first step on his journey:

I was baptized by the Rev. Courtney, Bishop of Nova Scotia, and in youthful days was an ardent high churchman, but I went from that emotionalism to Christian Science, then to Unity, and finally to Zen and Buddhism before I awoke from the dream of person and discovered that I AM as awareness was the object of the search. It had always been with me. I was too wrapped up in personal belief to see it.

Journal 19, 17 Aug 1987

David acted in plays in high school—the Trinity School in New York, graduating in 1917—and intended to study acting in college. George heatedly opposed and forbad this, although he had dabbled in acting himself as a young man. Instead, David went to the University of Toronto to study forestry—a subject that interested him because of his love of nature and the outdoors.

In 1919, likely on a summer break, David went to England to visit relatives. While there, at some point, he met Jiddu Krishnamurti. Krishnamurti, now 24 years old, had been brought to England from India as a young boy by the Theosophical Society, which considered him the new world teacher. The charismatic Krishnamurti impressed David with his view of all life being equally sacred.

I recall at age 19, Krishnamurti said to me, "Kill as little as possible." After that, I saw that even as we walked, the ants on the pavement were stepped over without knowing. "Kill as little as possible," and never with intent or passion. Where God is, there are no divisions such as small or large, greater or greatest. Nothing in God's universe is picayune or tremendous; all is sacred being.

Journal 1, 28 May 1978

However the meeting took place, a friendship developed, and this likely had great implications for David actively to question his participation in organized religion and to analyze the beliefs he had accepted without thought.

> I was brought into a world still severely under the influence of what is known as the Victorian era and a family deeply involved in the high Anglican Church. Not until the twenties was even a question in mind or a smidgen of doubt sowed in the heart. It was another twenty years before the first suggestion of the traps I lived in was made clear, and it came not from any book but out of the agony of misunderstandings, which I knew I had to escape from or be done in by.
>
> Journal 13, 1 Apr 1985

Their contact continued into the 1930s in Hollywood. One observer quotes a friend of David's as saying that they lived together for a time early in David's Hollywood sojourn. ("David Manners, The Final Interview, Part 2," by Rick McKay, www.rickmckay.com.) For some reason, the friendship evidently came to a bitter end, crushing David emotionally, with Krishnamurti refusing to recognize him again. In a letter to William Samuel, dated 12 May 1987, David notes with some irony:

> Krishnamurti's last words to mankind are, "Be absolutely alert without effort." I have said it differently and so have you. I was interested to know he didn't arrive at understanding until 1947—10 years after my association with him in Hollywood. I'm sure I was no help!"

But long before those events, David returned to college from his visit to England in 1919. Studying forestry was acceptable to George Acklom, so he paid David's college bills. David loved the outdoors, but he loved acting, too, and soon began following that pursuit in Toronto. Although speculation, just as meeting Krishnamurti might have begun David's questioning of organized religion, perhaps the friendship set him to question other aspects of his life, such as pursing acting. At any rate, around the end of 1920, George found out that David was acting at the Hart House Theatre in Toronto, and he stopped supporting David. David continued in college for a bit, but he eventually dropped out— because of poor grades as much as lack of support. Adrift, David returned home to New York City.

Coming back to New York only placed him closer to Broadway and the lure of the footlights.

Bright lights, dark shadows

When I was older, I went seeking in the world for a father I could love and who would love me. I found those who wanted the body but not a son. I never found that Daddy. I still feel cheated.

Journal 17, 5 Nov 1986

After returning from Toronto, David couldn't resist acting, and perhaps couldn't resist defying his father. By 1924, he had joined Basil Sydney's Touring Company, and he had performed in three plays. Also in 1924, under the name Michael Dawn, he appeared with Helen Hayes in Dancing Mothers, which ran for almost a year on Broadway at the Booth Theatre. Later, he joined Eva Le Gallienne's Civic Repertory Theatre. From this time until 1927, David met people in the theatre world, among them director George Cukor and writer Edmund Goulding, who would later play roles in his success in Hollywood.

David was now a young man who had experienced living away from home, but the time away from his father while David lived in Toronto hadn't eased the tension between them. David still carried the literal and metaphoric scars of his childhood. The schism with his father affected David throughout his life, although some kind of truce and understanding was reached before George died in 1954. "The bloody beatings didn't heal until George was about to pass" but "in those (early) days (I) would have gladly shot (my) father." (letter to William Samuel, 6 Jul 1987)

In his journals, on days when the memories were overwhelming, David would wonder how his relationship with his father and mother might have affected his sexuality.

> Does or did G(eorge) ever understand his son? Did he realize what happened to turn him the other way? Was it his seeking for a father to love? Was it a mother who was jealous of all women and girls and warned her son against involvement? Was it she who idealized men who influenced her son? Do I understand what happened? Or was it ever present from birth—the mix-up? Does all this really matter at all? This is the question. Somehow I feel it has something to do with the experience and is predetermined as necessary. I wonder, shall I ever know?
> Journal 27, 9 June 1992

David struggled with accepting his sexuality, alternately not caring who knew and then reburying the secret. The subject occupies occasional journal entries into his 90s. However, this entry from 1985 shows that David also felt the reality of his sexuality served a purpose, helping along his journey to wonder.

> There is a reason not recognized for the so-called society of

the unwanted—the odd people who seem to be out of step with the ordinary and who are labeled queer and gay and homo and all that. In myself, I see what has been behind all this, far behind the psychologists' definitions of father seeking or mother seeking as the case may be. It is, or has been for me, the purpose of awakening to Truth. Perhaps the man who is uninvolved with family, children, and grandchildren is more likely to see, to yearn, and to discover. And I may be here making excuses or trying to find an excuse for myself. I don't know, but I do feel there is a purpose behind every facet of life no matter what it appears to be.

Journal 13, 5 Feb 1985

Still the time in New York in the 1920s (and in David's twenties) was exhilarating. David was finally an actor being paid to act in the New York theatre. To supplement his income, David worked as an antiques and art dealer at Durlacher's Gallery, just off 5th Avenue on 54th Street. This position took him to England fourteen times in five years. On his last trip in 1928, he became seriously ill with pneumonia. The cure was to go west to Arizona.

Breaking in, breaking through

As a young man, Krishnamurti told me the power of reality would destroy me if I am not ready.

Journal 9, 4 Apr 1983

David found work on a dude ranch as a guide, and for a time, he was one of hundreds of crew members working to build the Arizona Biltmore Resort, which was designed by Frank Lloyd Wright and student Albert Chase McArthur. In *Look Through,* the "Dreamer Awakes" section, David describes how working to exhaustion in the desert and then being alone with himself brought about the "first stirrings of the Self," which in Krishnamurti's term were the first stirrings of reality for David.

While in Arizona, David met Susanne Bushnell, granddaughter of Asa Bushnell, former governor of Ohio. The beautiful and bright (she attended the Finch School in Versailles, France) socialite's engagement to David was announced in the New York Times on 24 April 1929. They were married in June. The newlyweds planned to stop in California on their way to Hawaii, where a relative of Suzanne's had promised David a job on a sugar plantation.

A stopover in Los Angeles, which was to last a few weeks, became permanent. David met up with old friends from New York, and as many have told, including David, he was "discovered" at a party by the director James Whale, who was casting Journey's End, a popular play about existing in the trenches in World War I. Whale is chiefly remembered as director of the horror films Frankenstein (1931), Invisible Man (1933), and Bride of Frankenstein (1935). David tested for the part of Raleigh, a part many actors wanted. The part fell into David's hands.

David tells this version of the story in this dramatic (perhaps overly so) and extensive journal entry.

> Perhaps you don't see that I too have been lost in that dark place of miserable personal sense with loss of a desired one who had deserted, loss of employment, and loss of friends. Because I couldn't take it anymore, I decided death was preferable to further loneliness, sickness, anger, and heartache. Finally, I asked for help. I got down on the floor and stretched out and held a loaded gun to my temple. A little pressure of the finger on the trigger and it would be over, so I thought. But there was doubt. It was this innate doubt that forced out a plea, "Father, if there is any purpose in this vale of misery, show it to me now."

Sounds like blackmail, doesn't it? Maybe the Father should have turned away in disgust, but Love understands and never turns away. What came to that foolish man was a question, "Before you do it, aren't you curious to see what your life would have been like? Wouldn't you like to see what you're going to miss?"

It was true. I did want to see what might have been, and as I lay there wondering, the telephone rang. I left the gun on the floor and answered. It was an acquaintance who told me that the Fox Studio was combing the town for fellows who could speak like an Englishman. It was a war film, and he had given my name to the assistant director. He hoped I didn't mind.

Mind? I minded nothing. I had nothing to lose. I'd do anything. We made a date to meet the next day and go to the studio. Little did I know, but it was the beginning of a new career and new interests, new people, a whole new life in which the chain of events was all leading the man to a great need for the understanding of consciousness, being, life—the way out of the deep shadow into sunlight.

Journal 20, 2 Feb 1988

Two days later, another journal entry continues this story. What would seem to be a path to happiness, for David, turns into a fast lane to nowhere.

But wasn't your new life the way out of darkness? That's the illusion, you see. I found the same problems in that new life that I had before, and even more so. They were stepped up, more passion, more sex, more desertion, more aches. Oh yes, there was money, physical comfort, and three meals a day, drink, and drugs, but no paradise, no Eden.

The search went on, and all the while the prayer for help, for illumination continued. Books there were, great books, all about the freedom I craved. I read and I thought and to a degree I understood, but the darkness around me was as deep as ever.

Journal 20, 4 Feb 1988

As David's Hollywood career was advancing, his marriage to Suzanne was floundering. Reports were that her family did not approve of acting as a career for her husband. In April 1930, they were listed in the United States Census as still living together, but soon after, she filed to annul the marriage and moved back to New York. She remarried on 9 May 1931 to Wallace Wesley Seymour and settled in Montclair, NJ.

But Rauff de Ryther Daun Acklom began a new life, too, as David Joseph Manners, taking his mother's maiden name for his new identity. He would legally adopt this name, as he would the United States, applying in 1932 to become a citizen (finalized in 1935).

Fame and infamy

During the years of the 30s and 40s in the full flush of life, I was a prisoner, imprisoned by myself and I never really enjoyed the many wonders of the world. How many of us are self-incarcerated?

Journal 17, 6 Oct 1986

David, now single and seemingly rescued from despair by New York friends in Hollywood, makes *Journey's End*. The part of 19-year-old Raleigh, earns him an instant reputation as a rising star. It also begins David's long list of roles in which he plays someone younger than himself, characterized by reviewers as "juvenile" parts. His continually being cast in these parts reached its point of absurdity when at 35 David played the ill-fated 21-year-old Edwin Drood in *The Mystery of Edwin Drood* (1935).

With the success of *Journey's End,* the Hollywood studio star machine took over, and David had to participate in public relations campaigns, photo sessions, and fan magazine interviews, but the object of these interviews was a person who did not actually exist.

> What is David Manners? He is something made up. I made him up out of whole cloth. With the help of family, friends, acquaintances, employers, and the world in general, that appearance is all made up of thought, data, concepts, names, dreams, and so on and is nothing lasting at all. He is a fraud, a synthetic thing. But there is something there, and it is the fact of his being aware, the fact of his consciousness, and that fact is all that is real.
>
> Journal 7, 3 Aug 1982

Of course, the Hollywood press connived with studio press agents to create an image for an actor. Here is just one example of the two working together to establish an image for David:

> Most ambitious of the cinema twains, it would seem is David Manners. In a single day, he was seen lunching with Peggy Fears, swimming with Bessie Lasley, and dining with the Countess di Frasso.
>
> *Los Angeles Evening Herald Express,* 29 June 1933

The publicity machine cast David as a handsome, eligible young man. But the invasive questions asked by the fan magazines and the need to give them a good story contrasted with what David thought was important, which was his work in a film not his personality. David disliked the focus on the ego and on image. He was also irritated at having to try to satisfy the demands of publicity while keeping his personal life separate and a secret. Increasingly, that public persona of David Manners was in conflict with his personal goals and interests. Nevertheless, personal information would come out in interviews. An example is the article "What Kind of an Actor Am I, Asks Manners" (14 Aug 1932, Los Angeles Record), which reported that:

> David is a "nice" person himself. As wholesome and decent as possible. He lives with his mother in a modest home with a wide lawn, nestling among the Hollywood hills. He is sensitive and a dreamer. He nurses a secret yearning to write—and has written some very nice things, which he keeps hidden away in a desk drawer. He reads books on metaphysics, but he doesn't talk about it. He says he is not in love—but he blushes when he says it—so how can you tell?

David worked with many leading ladies, including Helen Chandler, Katharine Hepburn, Loretta Young, Barbara Stanwyck, Kay Francis, Claudette Colbert, Constance Bennett, Myrna Loy, and Carole Lombard. As with many other actors, David was the subject of rumors about which starlet he was involved with. So, "dates" were arranged and were covered by the press, all of which became part of the job. Keeping up with the demands of fans also became part of the job. By 1935, his fan club counted 200,000 members, and four secretaries handled the correspondence. His popularity was so high, he was one of the first 100 actors to have a star on Hollywood Boulevard. (Years later, street construction removed the star and it was not replaced.) David always took time for fans then and well into his 80s, when he was signing publicity photos sent by new generations of fans.

> Mail comes from West Germany—imagine! Young fans of old movies sending photos to be autographed. Who said, "You should live so long"? I wonder. Ah, if those kids only knew what had happened to that actor.
>   Letter to William Samuel, 11 Mar 1986

For directors, David worked with some of the best: Frank Capra, George Cukor, Karl Freund, James Whale, and William Dieterle. Some of his more artistically successful films include *Journey's End, The Millionaire* (1931), *The Miracle Woman* (1931), *The Last Flight* (1931), *A Bill of Divorcement* (1932), and *Roman Scandals* (1933).

But it is for the horror films that he is remembered by the average filmgoer: *Dracula* (1931), *The Mummy* (1932), *The Black Cat* (1934), and, recently because of its appearance on DVD, *Death Kiss* (1932). (For an excellent review of David's film career, see John Norris's web site, www.davidmanners.com.)

First National Pictures (later owned by Warner Brothers Studios) held David's contract, but the company also loaned him (at a profit) to other studios, including Universal, Paramount, Fox, United Artists, and Columbia, until 1933 when David ended his contract and freelanced as an independent actor. As a freelancer, he instead would get the money that had gone to First National and Warner Brothers for loaning him to other studios. And David worked at a rapid rate from 1930 into 1936, making 39 films in that time. Although he valued his success, he also found it somewhat empty.

There was a time when the urge in living was to prove something to the temporal powers of world-man—to have them say, "Well done. You are an artist, and we can sell you and make money for you." This is no longer an urge. I have no wish left to prove anything to anybody, and I am content to be, to wait, to be aware of the grandeur here— the wonder here.

Journal 10, 5 Sep 1983

David's individuality surfaced off camera when he took control of his career. He was a founding member of the Screen Actors Guild, and he was known in the film community as professional, dependable, and bankable. In spite of his success, or perhaps because of it, David began to turn away from Hollywood. By 1933, whenever he could, David was off to Apple Valley, near Victorville, California. There, at Rancho Yucca Loma, David built a small adobe house, the site of his next great awakening.

Every time you say "I am miserable, ill, in pain," and so on you build your prison walls thicker and thicker. When I was in this limited state of mind in the 30s believing I had ulcers and locked myself away afraid of food, afraid of everything, and especially of dying, I came to my senses one day and realized I might better be dead than live a life of despair.

It was at this moment of decision to go and do all those things I pictured would kill me that I was miraculously healed. Man cannot live to himself and for himself, worrying about himself. This is death; this is hell. He must serve and help others. He must give himself away to live.

Journal 5, 8 Apr 1980

Rancho Yucca Loma—a home at last

David had met Gwen Boynton Behr in New York City sometime before 1928. She was the daughter of Dr. Catherine Boynton, a psychiatrist, and through Gwen, David heard of her mother's Rancho Yucca Loma. Boynton had purchased property there in 1917 to start a psychiatric facility. Her plan was for her patients to recuperate through the beauty and solitude of the high Mojave. Eventually, over 1,000 acres formed the ranch, and adobe cottages composed the compound. In the 1920s, Hollywood discovered Yucca Loma as a guest ranch, and the famous came to escape the looney world of stardom. The guest ranch was known and appreciated for keeping secrets and keeping the press away.

From 1933 to 1936, the Hollywood press carried short items about David escaping to Victorville and Yucca Loma in the Mojave Desert whenever he finished a picture and wasn't going directly into another one. David became a partial owner of the ranch in 1933 and began building a house there that same year. He would move there permanently after *A Woman Rebels* (1936), starring Katharine Hepburn, became his unplanned last film.

David, tantalizingly, at the beginning of *Look Through* explained why he left Hollywood.

> I suppose all seekers for Shangri-La did not in those days miss a chance of going to Hollywood, though few found the instant success that I did. But a very few years of movie making were enough for me. Wealth and a certain notoriety did not satisfy the inner hunger. When the chance came, I was off again and did the unforgivable thing of stepping out and away from sharing stardom with a big lady star, which I soon discovered by the venom which poured out after my departure was not the correct thing to do.

That "big lady star" was Joan Crawford. The list of leading ladies David acted with did not include her, and she was determined that it would. David's reputation was one of solid performance that never upstaged the lead actress. David told Rachel Samuel (sometime in the 1980s) that he finally agreed to be in a Joan Crawford starring vehicle, although he knew it would be difficult because the two were not friendly. It seems David had also refused over the years to accompany her on those studio "dates."

As David told Rachel, the first day working on the film brought the two stars to the soundstage, and in front of the crew, Joan released a torrent of abuse against David about whose picture this was, how he had ignored her over the years, and choice bits about his personal life. David claimed to have said nothing, left the sound stage, and never worked in Hollywood again. Sources do not note the film's title, but of Joan's two films in 1936, *The Gorgeous Hussey* and *Love on the Run,* it is the second film that more closely resembles the plot of David's usual characters and films. Although it doesn't prove the film was the one involved, *Love on the Run* was released one month after *A Woman Rebels.*

David, although glad to leave Hollywood, reflected on walking away from what had been so easily given to him.

> I see youngsters today struggling to find recognition in the world of ability and art, and I see how so much was given to me and made easy and so much thrown away unappreciated and I wonder at the kindness of fate or whatever to an unappreciating bastard.
> Letter to William Samuel, undated 1983

After moving to Yucca Loma, he designed and built more cottages for guests, helped run the ranch, worked on his two novels, and studied Truth authors. Catherine Boynton, whom David called Kate, and Helen Freedman, a resident at the ranch, started him on the path of Christian Science, Unity, and Religious Science, and they offered care, comfort, and advice to David, who was ill and had become fragile from the pressures of Hollywood.

> I see the purpose for the miserable creature I was. There was no out but to surrender all the personal life and let go, let be. Kate knew the possibility was there, and that's why I was put up with. Kate knew the real, and she took a chance on D. It was her belief that made the future secure and gave me the time for study.
>
> Journal 22, 29 Jul 1989

For several years, life at Yucca Loma was not easy for David. He was beset with terrible pain from a duodenal ulcer, and he suffered at the criticism of leaving Hollywood. He also suffered from conflict over his sexuality and his yearning for spiritual sustenance and release. At times, he lived almost as a recluse in his cottage. But, as time went on, David did get healthier and joined fully in ranch life.

> Oh, the Easters on the Rancho! What a do! David wore all white. I guess he thought he was one of the Essenes or a guiding angel. He decorated his house with flowers and candlelight, served coffee and Danish to the early risers who went to the knoll to see the sun rise. He also played symphonic music on the great Scott machine, the first with three speakers and a hi-fi sound.
>
> Letter to William Samuel, 19 April 1987

He also completed and published his two novels, *Convenient Season* (published in 1941 by E. P. Dutton, but begun earlier during his Hollywood days) and *Under Running Laughter* (1943, Dutton). A third novel went unpublished because of the paper shortage during the later stages of World War II. He also managed to do his bit for the war effort.

In '42 [World War II—ed], I was turned down again—flat feet and color ignorance, as well as duodenal ulcer. [David had been turned down for service in World War I also—ed.] That was a dark year in D's life. I was self-rejected, asocial, and sick of the stomach, but I did take the night shift at running the USO and running the ranch all day to free Gwen for Red Cross duty. I also directed a roaring comedy for the Special Service group at George Air Force Base [Victorville Army Air Field at the time—ed], which was a big hit with the base. A really mad outcome of all this attempt at compensation for rejection was a citation at the war's end from Mr. Roosevelt for services rendered.

Letter to William Samuel, 17 Oct 1987

With men returning home at the end of World War II, workers were available again at the ranch. David returned to New York for an extended visit with his parents in Hastings on Hudson. From a chance meeting, agent Alan Brock coaxed him back to Broadway.

Brock recognized David in the congregation attending Christmas Eve mass. Brock convinced David to consider playing Wing Commander Hern in the cast of *Truckline Café* (1946), a play if judged by the cast, writer, and producer should have been a success. Written by Maxwell Anderson, produced by Elia Kazan, with a cast that included Marlon Brando (in his second Broadway role), Karl Malden, and Kevin McCarthy, the play lasted for just 13 performances. About the psychological effects of World War II on soldiers, *Truckline Café* is remembered mostly for Brando's performance—and his character didn't enter until the third act. Critics voted him Broadway's Most Promising Actor for 1946.

David followed this disappointment with an Agatha Christie play, *Hidden Horizon,* opposite Diana Barrymore. He predicted the play would fail miserably, and it did, lasting 12 performances. But David went from this play into summer stock, performing in *The Male Animal.* From there, he joined the successful touring production of *Lady Windemere's Fan.* After over 500 performances, the run ended in June 1948.

David had now been away from his beloved ranch for two years. The return home, importantly, changed David's life again. David found the man who would be his companion for the next 30 years, or rather a friend found him for David.

> A beloved mutual friend, Helen Freeman, brought Bill Mercer to our desert home in the summer of 1948—thirty years ago. Immediately, Bill and I recognized that we spoke the same language and were on the same path of self-discovery. For thirty years, we worked and studied together, laughed and prayed. A friend once said Bill and David are like the Jonathan and David of the Bible story.
>
> Journal 2, 3 Oct 1978

Frederic William Mercer was a playwright and screenwriter, 18 years David's junior, and was as gregarious as David was reserved. Bill was the handy one, fixing and decorating the places they lived together. In Bill, David found the companion and mate he had searched so long for, someone who shared his quest for spiritual truth.

Yucca Loma was David's and Bill's home until 1954, when the primary co-owner Gwen Behr died. Her mother, Catherine Boynton, had died in 1949. Gwen left the ranch to David and her stepfather. He and David kept the ranch going for a time, but they reluctantly decided to sell in 1956. David used his sizable proceeds to purchase a house on the ocean in Pacific Palisades. Except for David's house, the ranch cottages and buildings were torn down because of then present-day building code violations. A subdivision took their place. Today, David's former home at what was Yucca Loma is still standing.

The over 20 years David spent at Yucca Loma were a time of self-imposed aloneness and joyful camaraderie, a time of spiritual searching and earthly connection, a time of losing one identity and assuming a new one. David's journey had taken him from Hollywood to the Mojave Desert and then to Pacific Palisades. The time he spent living at each location changed him, but he was still not reaching the breakthrough he sought.

When I was a young man, I went to the desert, built myself an austere little house of adobe and tile, and there I expected to find all the answers and to become a holy man.

Twenty-five years later, I was still without answers and still far from being a man at peace or of peace. It was then I recalled the words of a wise young friend who, as I departed on the quest from life as an actor to life as a recluse, said, "You'll never find it in the desert!"

This was the truth. I never found it in any geographical spot. . . .I had searched everywhere in man, in woman, in systems, in solitude, in books, in personal love and found nothing but sorrow. Now, I see what I missed. Now, I live here as this wonder I AM that is Life being Life. Home is where I am. What I used to think of as God or Great Spirit out there somewhere is now right here all around.

Journal 10, 4 Dec 1983

A journey shared, a journey alone

David and Bill lived at 1224 Chautauqua in Pacific Palisades, overlooking Will Rogers State Park. For 21 years, the house was another sanctuary for David and a happy home full of reading, gardening, writing, and visits from old friends. The pair was active socially in the neighborhood, and David hadn't lost touch with Hollywood friends, many of whom had been guests at Yucca Loma. He and Bill often attended parties at George Cukor's home too.

For several years in the 1960s, David honed his considerable artistic talents with painting lessons from Lee Mullican, an internationally known West Coast modernist and professor at UCLA. David published Look Through in 1971 and a second edition in 1978. He wrote other metaphysical manuscripts and more fiction, but he often destroyed complete manuscripts because he felt they were naïve or of little value. One work of fiction, *The Leading Man,* went through four major drafts and was even reviewed by two editors, but David destroyed all copies in 1987. In journal entries, he indicated that the novel dealt frankly with 1930s Hollywood and included a gay leading character.

Occasionally, David granted interviews to those doing research on former Hollywood colleagues, but he disliked reliving the past. Although he generously signed publicity stills sent to him, he wanted no part in glorifying the flickering images of someone who in David's opinion only existed in the world of Hollywood myth making. That isn't to say that he wasn't proud of his acting work and didn't appreciate what Hollywood enabled him to do with the rest of his life. It was just that he preferred to live in the present.

David sold the house on Chautauqua in 1978 because of a sour deal with a stock trader.

> Bill and I were taken to the cleaners once by a sharp stockbroker whom we believed in and who demolished our savings of $68,000—all of it. That's why we had to sell the house there. It was all that was left, and miraculously it sold at twice the price we expected and made Santa Barbara possible. Since that experience, I confine my activities to savings only—no more stock market!
> Letter to William Samuel, 6 Feb 1984

He and Bill moved to a condo in Montecito, near Santa Barbara, California. The move proved a hardship on Bill, whose health had not been robust since a car accident in the 1950s at Yucca Loma. On 27 August 1978, at age 60, Bill died in his sleep of a heart attack. David bore his grief through his metaphysical beliefs, but there was no denying the great loss he felt. The following two entries are from David to Bill.

> Bill M. and I are one now and eternally. ...Wait a little for me Bill. I'll be there or here with you in Paradise. You have been of great riches to me and still are the richest thing in my life. Thank you for Being. Friend of my heart!
> Journal 2, 27 Aug 1978

> A hard day. Bill, I have to go right back to the beginning. I've lost my way in sorrow and self-pity missing you, the visible you. Now I have to go back to asking who am I? Who are you? What is going on? Where am I? I was strong, I said, and now I am weak. I cannot walk alone. Or can I? Yes, I have to; there's no other way. I must walk on. I must

know how to reach you. You know of the love I bear. You must know. Be with me as the Light you are.

Journal 2, 31 Aug 1978

David stayed at the condo in Montecito until 1984, when he moved to Santa Barbara and a smaller apartment. At 84, he wanted less space to take care of and fewer possessions. He continued to write in the journals and wrote many letters to friends. In 1986, David acquired a computer and taught himself the workings of word processing in the modern age. In 1987, he published Awakening from the Dream of Me. That year, he moved to Wood Glen Hall, a retirement facility.

The first Christmas at Wood Glen Hall, however, rekindled memories of Bill.

Tinsel time is here again with its colored balls and fairie lights. It brings Bill M back strong with his love of décor. He was a Christmas Child if ever there was one. I wish you could have seen the dining table at the ranch, a white tablecloth with red ribbons and all along the center miniature reindeer pulling a loaded sleigh and a fat Santa. Big red candles, greens, desert holly, and wreaths everywhere (handmade). Ah, so. I guess Christmas is a time of memories.

Letter to William Samuel, 8 Dec 1987

At Wood Glen Hall, David could leave cooking and the household cares to the staff and enjoy his time as he pleased, writing his quarterly metaphysical newsletter, recording tapes to further his message, and working in his journals. But by 1992, he needed more personalized care, so he moved to Marge Mason's Montecito Senior Care facility. The home-based facility emphasized nutrition and activities in a serene garden setting. David enjoyed Marge's care until 1996 when his frailties required the help of a skilled nursing staff, so he moved to Valle Verde Health Care in Santa Barbara.

David continued steady correspondence with friends, even getting a fax machine for more instant communication. But the pains of old age continued their march as David's health declined. In 1998, so near the Christmas time he fondly remembered, David died on 23 December of cardiac arrest.

In 1999, on David's birthday, his niece Patricia Bergen, her children, and Rick McKay, a film producer and writer who had become friends with David after interviewing him, met on the grounds of David's former home at Yucca Loma. The young couple who then owned the house agreed that David should come home. David's ashes were scattered at his beloved adobe cottage in the Mojave Desert.

> Somehow, sweetly, I have been shepherded right from the outset. How else could you have found Catherine and her place on the desert? How else could you have been picked out of a hopeless mess and given Journey's End? How could you walk away from all that and be taken care of? Never have I had to labor. Bill and the money were gifts. The house on Chautauqua was a gift, and the way I got here today—always taken care of. Oh, wondrousness. Proof you want? All the life of this one is proof. I have lived the proof. At last, I know where the shepherd is. Right here, as all, as this one. Once these were words; now there is Light. Faith is built on hope and trust, but knowing is something else.
>
> Journal 23, 21 Feb 1990

The wonder within

"How did enlightenment finally come to you?" David heard this question many times when he engaged others who were curious about his ideas and his books.

> There was no sudden engulfment in light. It was little by little, a flash here, a glimpse there, but ever more than enough to keep me at it. I found struggling and wanting had to go, along with the sense of a personal me. I saw that dying to the personal sense of life was necessary for an experience of lasting peace.
>
> Over a period of some 40 years of living, there grew understanding and an ability to take the step out of personal living into the vast and infinite region of Is-ness. No, it was not an easy path. I don't feel it is really easy for anyone, but as ego-care dies, Love is born.
>
> Journal 20, 5 Feb 1988

Through his study of many Eastern and Western philosophies, and then living the principles that touched him most, David came to see that God or Spirit—terms were not important—is within and always available to everyone.

> No tools, no money, no travel, no teacher, no group, no organization is needed. The ultimate is here, and it is free and open to everyone. No identification card is needed, no scroll of great deeds or list of failures. Come as you are, naked of the world's judgments.
>
> Journal 6, 27 Jan 1982

Whichever role resonates with you for David Manners . . . actor, author, metaphysician, or philosopher . . . look through the labels to see the man who sought Truth, found it for himself, and so wanted to share it with others.

> If the Truth that is hidden here comes through to you, say it secretly in your own words and experience the celebration of the heart.

Journal 17, 4 Nov 1986

Part 2

Excerpts from the newsletters

What you really are

A glimpse of awareness reveals what you really are. You really are both the seen and unseen. You are light, not only the light that illumines this paper you read, but the Light of which the word light is but an image or reflection. This glimpse of awareness is a flash of infinite glory that shows the very presence of what is called God.

Here is infinite forgiveness calling you to come and consciously be the wonder that life is. It is an experience without words, an invitation to behold truth and behold infinite and ineffable love.

Awareness is the gateway to wondrous living that reveals the secret of healing—the body and spirit are one. As you understand that you are not a separate person but that you are united with all life, this conscious awareness liberates you from the burden of past errors, and you begin to live openly, joyfully, and fearlessly as the Child of almighty Being that you truly are.

Without definitions

God expresses in infinite form, color, and modes of communication. All have their place and purpose. Never feel thwarted by a term that says nothing to you because of your conditioning. Terms are as individual as you are, as the I AM is. Does the term speak to your I AM? If not discard it, or better still, find your own term.

In the higher stages of unfoldment, terms can be discarded altogether and only the experience of Being is sufficient. I have witnessed so much consternation over terms and teachers. I decided long ago to use any term from whatever source that fits the individual need. It is understanding not words that count.

Therefore, be of open mind and heart. The heart has its own language, a wordless one that cuts through all differences to infinitude. Where the heart knows, all arguments, all "shalls," disappear. One all-encompassing divine sound is heard. Within pure awareness, where no concept at all exists, is a universe without dimension, without time or space or directions. This is the universe of Spirit. It is always here and now as the awareness or consciousness we are.

You might ask, what is Spirit? One might as well ask for a definition of God. Who can give it? We know it as the motivating creative power, an unlimited energy that is omnipresent, omniscient, and omnipotent. But no one can name it or define it. Our words and ways are finite and God-Spirit is infinite. This presence of infinite love, this almighty and unnamable one, is all as all. This conscious awareness tells us of the Presence that is beyond all human condition of inside or outside and all dualities.

We can understand the magnitude of this Is-ness we all partake of as Life, but we cannot define it or in anyway separate it from the wonder of what we are. The dimensionless, unbound infinitude of that Is-ness simply is. And that is all that can be said. When we ask for definitions, we are trying to box in the indefinable and eternal to fit the human brain.

Each of us has a spark of the almighty fire that has been termed soul. In this life, the wise seek the companionship of Soul, for it is our salvation. It is our joy, our power, our energy, our inspiration. It is our way of transcending mortal existence and entering what Jesus called the Kingdom of Heaven.

The present wonder

I might believe I am nothing, have nothing, and know nothing. But wait! I exist, I am. This fact—this conscious awareness—is the only reality. The conscious awareness of I AM is the action of the almighty Being (God). How could I have lived so long and not have understood this obvious fact, this present wonder?

Understanding and experiencing the truth about I AM diminishes the power that the mortal, personal mind with its prejudices, violences, greed, and its separational judgments might have over the human creature.

Understanding truth gives to all mankind a new freedom, a new interest in and enjoyment of all the various aspects of living. As the beholder of God's infinite Being, even in a limited manner, I am so much more than I ever dreamed.

As I keep attentive to this wonderful fact, living expands. I see now that it is entirely up to me whether I live in darkness or in light. I choose to be in the light of understanding. How about you?

Nothing can ever be revealed to a mind of personal sense. A conditioned mentality can struggle endlessly and find only its own conditioned state. So, what is the answer? Be still and know that the conscious awareness of I AM is the activity of God's immortal and ineffable Mind.

What was present before the conditioning began? The unadulterated little child is naturally aware and fascinated by the wonder of that into which it is born. As the child grows older, the conditioning begins and the early simplicity is gradually covered over and forgotten.

Now, I do not mean to imply that there are two human minds, one clear and pure and the other a bag full of errors. There is only one perfect awareness, such as the mind of the little child, but we muddy it with false beliefs of a personal sense.

The pure, happy beholding of the little child is still present waiting to be rediscovered or uncovered. And what do you suppose it is that begins the rediscovery? Isn't it the pain, sorrow, sickness, loneliness, darkness, and despair that personal sense has led us into? It is the very thing that stimulates a desire and need to be free of it. We see at last that to be wholly alive there has to be peace through understanding.

And what beats the heart, digests the food, and activates the brain without any direction of personal mind? That which blooms the rose and the dandelion, leafs the tree, and grows the seed that in turn produces the lion cub and the infant man is Mind in action. Thus, we live in and as wonder.

These words I write are never the understanding. The words are the arrows that point the way. But do not stand worshipping the arrows. Enter the gate where language is not, where there are no pros and cons. In the stillness, be at the point of perfect balance, where no human image is. It is there that you are in the present wonder.

Point of balance

More and more clearly I see the importance of being free of outward expressions, free of the seeking and expecting to find one's reality in books or through gurus or through anyone else. There is no short circuit or short cut. Man has to recognize this principle of his being: He already is the very wonder that he seeks to be.

The problem seems to be in confusing the personal sense of man with the reality that his being is. Only through leaving the personal sense or conditioned person in the mire of his error where he usually is, and stepping away into boundlessness where thought and imaging are not, can one see clearly the wonder that man, as life, really is.

Man has gone—and is going—endlessly outward, with more inventions, more complexities, more machines. He has lost touch with the simple awareness that is present every moment of life as everything he does, in every movement and every breath he takes.

Man as a rule is so deeply involved with how to sate his appetites for sex, wealth, temporal power, and all the various wants of his personal sense that he does not see that he is ever building a thicker and more impenetrable cocoon around himself.

Only the glowing warmth of Truth revealed can free man from his husk and transform him. That truth is here present. It has always been so. It takes only his awakening from the dream, the belief that he is a mortal. It takes only a question: Who built the wretched web that holds him prisoner? Man did.

For generations on end, he has been building it with what he calls "improvements" in living, which are nothing more than the inventing of ever more and more distractions to fill the void in his heart. But that void, that ache, that yearning can never be filled with any outward invention or any organization for inner balm. Only when inward and outward are abandoned as no more than two extremes of the same problem is there discovery of balance, that divine point of perfect rest between the two deceptive extremes.

Love, like an infinite ocean, ever beats upon the walls of man's self-made defenses. But what is he defending against? What is he afraid of that he has to hide his precious person? If all he has is the person of senses, then he is lost for this person of senses is doomed from the moment of birth.

Why hold on to something always vulnerable to loss? The only purpose of the me-will is to expose its worthlessness. Being attached to it is hugging fool's gold to the breast.

No matter how strong is man's grip on it, it is bound to leave him, along with the dry husk or cocoon that is his conditioning and that he has believed is his life. The brilliance of truth dims what he is accustomed to regard as light. True Light is found here in the absence of me-sense where tensions simply do not exist.

At this point, this question inevitably arises: What are the benefits of relinquishing the me-sense? Only someone who is still defending and gripping that "precious" sense of person asks this question. The question reveals that the questioner has not yet discovered the wonder of a perfect balance.

Living the perfect balance of the liberated I is understanding that questions and answers are in the same category as good and evil and all other opposites. They have no real existence.

Living this understanding and being in perfect balance is a matter of self-discovery that is not done for us by books or by teaching, but ever is done by the one alone who is.

The reality of man has been dubbed the Spark, the Splendor, the Christ, the Eternal Spirit, the Child. By whatever name, the nameless One is ever present. Man, unaware, is everywhere crying for release from the straw dictator that holds him prisoner. Yet only a whisper, a single thrust of truth can inflame the thing of straw and destroy it, thus setting the beleaguered one free to discover his true life and real being.

So many in the world today are weary of the old patterns and are seeking escape. They are ready to relinquish the rule of the sense person that has brought nothing but anguish, illness, and ennui. Oh, encourage the weary to join the march, to claim true freedom, to claim the fire that is truly theirs.

Man is wonder. He is light. He is the untrammeled child he left behind in his quest for the sating of the senses and the desire for riches and power. That tranquil child still awaits release and recognition. Be as untrammeled as a little child at play and hear the sigh of gratitude. Let it all go and be free!

Understanding

Knowing truth does not come from university instruction or libraries. Man knows nothing of the cause called God. Man knows not what man is. When he has the courage to face the mystery he is and to live as mystery, then he is ready to begin understanding. An accumulation of worldly knowledge is the very barrier from which man must first step aside. Pride in mental acquisition can do nothing but defeat efforts in this respect.

Returning to the simplicity we had before human conditioning began is the first step toward understanding. From early days, we are taught that God is somewhere out there and that up there is heaven. Later, usually forced by the miseries of personal beliefs to look elsewhere, we begin to see the value in being still and listening.

I recall a mother's effort in teaching her children to say, "Our Father who art in heaven . . . ." Of course, heaven was somewhere up there in the sky. The church experience more or less confirmed it. It also taught that I was a miserable sinner but that God would forgive if I asked.

Thus, the great dichotomy took root in the child. The world was seen as good and evil. Even the children's stories were all based in this duality. No wonder it was hard going for the youngster. Some of us take a lifetime to return to the simplicity of the little child before teaching and conditioning built that sturdy shell called worldliness around us.

At last, and at first in brief glimpses, we discover we are already one with God as the conscious awareness we are. We discover that we were never anything else—that we could never be anything else—no matter how awful the appearance might be.

Greater than appearances

Where did the present idea of God come from? Isn't it also part of the conditioning put upon the child at the outset? Suppose there never had been a word taught about a God or cause or anything else on that topic, then how would you be expressing your deeper feelings today?

Go deep and see beyond and behind the teaching, the reading, and all the stuff passed on from elders. Let the human, conditioned mind go blank, be empty. In the stillness, are you not still aware of being? Whenever you are empty of thought, you are face to face with the original, timeless, conceptless fact of being. Listen, there is more.

The images in the eye of flesh tell that something must have caused this phenomenon. I look at the appearance of kinetic or animate energy, as well as static or inanimate energy, and I sense, I feel a sureness that tells me such images do not appear without a moving force, a reality, some unknown wonder that is the original cause. Honestly, I know nothing except that wonder is expressing as the very conscious awareness I AM.

Free of labels, there is no doubt that I am a mystery, and all the objective appearances of which I am aware are also a mystery. I cannot deny that I sense or am aware of a continuing presence far greater than the images I see. No matter how diligently I might want to erase this presence, it remains as I do, but it is infinitely greater than I am and all that I can perceive. It seems I am back where I began. I have come full circle and cannot yet get beyond the circle.

I observe a single cell out of which this body form grew and which is wholly related to an earthly or planetary nature. I see this also as the effect of some original cause in a particular environment that is compatible to the existing form. However, there is something else that appears to have a purpose behind its evolving forms as a means to some end or idea.

But what I sense is definitely not limited to the form in which I find myself. I have no proof whatever that sense is more than wish, but proofless, I know and feel something greater here than appears. This creates a wish to sing; it creates happiness without cause, and a trust, and a peace that is not of this world.

Again, I have no proof, other than the living of it. No matter how inspired an explanation, it is pointless to box the infinite into concepts. Let us be done with mental images. Let us live it and be glad.

The glory of oneness

In our business of social living, most of us are unaware that we are making life a series of separate things, people, and events. We see our employment as one thing. We see the garden and its chores as another. We see our body and its functions as separate. We see the neighbors, good ones and bad ones, also as separate, to say nothing of the planet and the galaxies of lights that we think of as "out there." And what about people of different color or those who do not speak our language?

Our lives are full of divisions, departments. And it is all a lie—a shallow seeing, a misinterpretation of life.

What can be done about this error that causes us to be victims of delusion and false beliefs? What good is there in loving the flowers in your garden and then turning away because the neighbor you dislike comes outside. We live in a silken cocoon of our own weaving and wonder why we get sick, depressed, and lonely. Perhaps we have too much of the material goodies of the world and no love, which is such a dangerous and ignorant way to live.

As said in Proverbs, " . . .with all your getting, get understanding." Only through seeing or understanding the divine unity of all forms, sizes, shapes, and sounds from the grasses of the field to the vastness of star-strewn space, all as conscious awareness, can we ever hope to live wholly.

It is common to wonder where the rapist, murderer, and thief belong, but if we see that such misguided creatures are the result of human conditioning even as our particular personal sense is also, we then recognize that essentially, as awareness, we are all one. Had our conditioning been similar, any one of us might have followed the identical patterns that imprison the felon.

The divisions of our world, which so many believe in, are the problems we all share. We, the peoples of the world, make them, but the purity of principle is unaffected. It can be neither darkened nor lightened. Principle ever remains perfect. The principle, the wonder we call awareness (God) is unaffected by the errors in man's personal sense of things.

Through the years of this life's living, I have discovered many ways of experiencing awareness, but the most helpful has been and is journal keeping. It is in the quiet hours, when stillness of the busy human mind comes easily, that the majesty and wonder of the Presence floods the being with its Self.

Such glimpses do not come all at once but come step by step from little glimpse to greater glimpse. It is not a doing, but rather it is a spontaneous happening of proportions that defeat any words about it. There is a flooding of love; love that is free of all opinions and judgments and that includes all. Infinite variety is sees as one, as Mind the source we call God. It is Mind beholding Mind.

The darkness that we wonder about so much merely delineates the onlyness and wonder of Light. There is purpose in the darknesses; they eventually draw all mankind back to the wonder of being and the awareness of the Presence of God as infinite, glorious wonder.

Discovery

It is not easy to be in the world and not of it. Most of us are obliged to carry on activities and associations that hold our attention, but some of us have discovered it is possible to work, talk, or whatever and also be constantly in awareness of Awareness itself. Yet, the temptation to slip into a pattern of nonattention and do nothing is always there. I know I am not here for such a purpose. If you also know this, then read on.

I find when things get rough, there is always something that feels as if a greatly beloved one is standing near awaiting recognition, demanding nothing, but always gently waiting. If I continue to ignore this present something, I am tense, unhappy, lonely, and I feel lost. Nothing pleases, and all feels in vain.

I expect many of us have experienced this and perhaps have found ways to ignore it. Since the first glimpse, years ago, of infinite wonder, I found I couldn't go on living and ignore it. Oh, for the bulk of a long life, I did ignore and was in hell, in the depth of the shadow, and it was that very hell that showed the way to walk out of that shadow.

At first, there were only moments of light, but once glimpsed, I had to go on learning to master the conditioned mind. I had to discover the blessing of relinquishment. It was not about doing something. It was an undoing, a learning of the value of being still.

There grew a deep need to be a master of the wandering mind, but such efforts were at first brief and far between. Now, there is a deep need to comply, which overrides all negation. I might liken it to the need of a lover to be ever near the loved one, a need to be in the presence of the something that is greater than I.

When one lives aware of the wonder of Awareness itself, one finds it difficult to understand how one could have delayed so long. It is as if one had kept the greatly loved ineffable One waiting. In indolent and deliberate ignorance, one has bent the knee to empty idols while that for which the heart has ever yearned continues to support the recreant. There is no greater joy and release from tension than to abandon and relinquish the yes-no, like-dislike world of opposites and be in union with this wonder that we are.

The voice of the reader shouts, "That's all very well for you, but how did you get this joy?" Another voice cries out, "I've heard this before, and none of it has done any good for me." The sobbing continues, "I'm lonely and sick. Where do I go? How can I find help?"

I never intended to do anything for a personal sense of me or to wave a wand and instantly transport everyone out of the dark shadows into Light. If you are sitting in the shade of a great tree and are beginning to feel cold and sick of shadow, isn't it usual to get up and walk out into the warm sunshine? Who can do it for you?

Shut up in a cocoon of personal self and personal self-pity, you are blind to the very wonder that gives you life, gives you the ability to cry out how sick and lonely you are. The caterpillar knows when it is the right moment to grow wings and force itself out of the cocoon into the wonder of a new freedom as a butterfly.

When things grow painful enough, you will find the way to sight and understanding and walk out into the Light. The warm Light you will find is not one that sets. There is no night with the wonder of conscious awareness. Therefore, give thanks for every dark moment that caused you to yearn deep enough that you asked the Father to show you the way.

This morning I sat in the sun, and I saw plainly that so many presume that the sunlight, the scene the eyes perceive, is going on out there, which isn't it at all. Nothing is going on out there. There is no out there. There is only the wonder conscious awareness is. Everything is going on right here and now as this wonder. How? How do you exist? How do you breathe? Are the senses of person so strong and the curtain of opposites so thick that you cannot see the very principle in operation that is your life?

Take a step away from the noisy, violent, painful life that you are in the habit of accepting as real. Take a step into the vast silence that surrounds. Be in that place of perfect balance between all extremes. It is natural and not difficult. Stop all trying and doing and simply listen. Here is consciousness, the wonder itself. Here is peace you have never experienced before. Here is happiness and ease that is new, all new. It is automatically and spontaneously expressed as living—unplanned and unexpected.

Belief versus Is-ness

What do we do with the great accumulated mass of conditioned thinking most of us have built around us and have lived in since childhood? I say do nothing. Walk away from it.

Sounds easy, doesn't it? First, of course, is the awareness of the accumulated mass and the unhappy results of it in man, which appear as crimes, hates, likes, dislikes, worry, fear, sicknesses, ad infinitum. Most of us live in the prison of our beliefs and cannot see any way out. But if there is a want, a real need to find a way, then "ask and ye shall receive." This is the beginning of walking away. But any reliance upon the world of mental imaging leads back to the world of the yea and nay dualities.

Awareness tells that where a negative appears, there is also a positive. A shadow, no matter how dark, could not exist without light. What is usually asked is how to break out of a negative situation or out of darkness. I was once asked to write a book on how to do this. The answer is as obvious as the answer to "how do I get up in the morning and go to breakfast?" I do it. So where's the book?

We are all Light—now and here and ever. To be aware of the mental mess is to be free of it. Awareness is all we need. Go back to the unimpaired happiness experienced as a seven-day-old child, a child with eyes filled with wonder. Existence is wonder, an unexplainable wonder. Let that wonder fill you. Enjoy the wonder of it all. Awareness is to be lived. If I could in some way share the free happiness in heart, I would. Maybe the sun does it by simply letting the light shine. If you are making a problem of it, forget it;

leave it alone. The problem could mean you simply are not ready.

It is incredible that so many of these man-creatures, as which we appear to be, simply take existence for granted. Life is a mystery. From the sperm and egg and growing into a sensed organism that talks about "my mind, my body, my house," and so on, where is the understanding that the sperm and egg were never a beginning? Where is the understanding that nothing in heaven or earth is mine? All in heaven and earth is only an effect of the whole ineffable wonder.

I stand at the back door looking down at the dandelion near the bottom step. We were told it is a dandelion, but I ask what is a dandelion? You might tell me it is a weed or give me a long botanical name, which still tells me nothing real. I am not asking for words, I am asking, what is it? All I know is it is a wonder even as I am.

I look up past the star suns into an infinity of space. I ask again, what is it? I get plenty of answers, some far more complicated than the botanical name of the dandelion, but still words, words, and more words, and again I know naught.

I am awed, not at the stars or space, but at this awareness, this wonder I AM. Without awareness there is no space, no stars, no black hole, and no one to observe. Do the names I call it make it any more understood? Never!

But there is something beyond words and senses deep within us that knows. The seven-day-old babe knows. It is the undwordable wonder that is the happiness I cannot explain. I need nothing else except to try to share it. How do I share it without a word? I know of no way but to enjoy it.

The still pool

In Oregon, somewhere between Crater Lake and Portland and on a less traveled road, I was driving through a forest of great redwoods. The forest floor was alive with ferns, small and large. On impulse, I turned the car and parked beside the road. I had to walk in the sweet twilight created by the trees. I walked carefully to avoid damaging the ferns, and that meant taking a wandering path through the trees.

Suddenly, I came upon a glade of light. In the center was a forest rain pool of clear water, unruffled by a breath of breeze. The pool, as still as a sheet of glass, reflected the surrounding forest and a bright patch of sky with its disorderly flow of cloudlets.

As I stood there watching, two birds swooped across, leaving not a trace on the surface of the pool. But there also was I, an image staring up, one man among the many reflected images. Before me on the surface of the pool was a duplicate world complete in every detail, a world free of even a trace of judgment, comment, comparison, or preference. The beauty of the scene held me. The surrounding silence was awesome.

Wordless, I knew that here where I stood I also was reflecting something I called a world, a universe, a wonder. I had never seen it before in its utterly pure state. Habitually, I had been smearing, distorting, discoloring my view in a way that prevented me from seeing anything as it was.

The usual ear that liked to listen to words and phrases, spoken or unspoken, was suddenly sealed. Stillness of an awesome nature took the stage and the man of human, conditioned sense ceased to exist. I was new.

Beyond the ear of flesh, I began to hear a tremendous song, something ineffable. I heard that the world man lives in is caused by the stick of judgment and belief that he uses to stir and muddy the pool. Man is seeking, but he will never see as long as he holds on to the stick and stirs. Only when he drops the stick and lets the pool be still can his images be true and he can begin to live.

Songs of the silence

In silence, music is heard that fills the heart with utter joy. This music has no notes and no instrument to play it. Mere words cannot hint at its beauty and sweetness. The purity of the empty page remains unstained by ink.

I lay down the pen and listen deeply, and then I hear the music. This music moves and swirls and yet it is still. Would that all could hear it. If heard, there would be no pain or fear, but only peace, a knowing and living of a mighty presence that is a love that sings, "Amen, Amen." Love knows all. No song goes unheard. Even the feeblest heart that cries, "I love, I love," remains forever inscribed within the wonder that pure awareness is.

Are there any wondrous words that can record the song the heart is singing? The answer comes as yet another question: Does the lover ever find the perfect word to tell his loved one what is in his heart? No, the lover stumbles, whispers, blurts, and his loved one always understands. The loved one knows the truth is not in any words and hears the song the heart is singing.

Forget words, and hear the soundless song that the beloved hears. Response is instant, and the knowing of it flows through every cell. There is never any doubt about what is true and what is false. Truth is ever with you, ever here, ever now. There is no other place or time. Awareness is.

All is ever present

It is common to wish that one could find the words to express the inexpressible. Much is known in the depths within that is of infinite quality and thus impossible to express finitely. It is experienced, a union with ineffable wonder is felt, but there is no proof other than the actual living of it. The one who yearns is still suffering from a belief in separation, of being apart, and such a one is prone to grief, loneliness, and emptiness. The one who is united yearns not, for he knows no real separation is possible.

There are those who ask, "How can we be sure this is true?" There is only one way to be sure. It is to live aware of the wonder that life and awareness are, the wonder that beingness is.

I have received letters from people who are suffering loneliness because of the loss of a loved one. The Nazarene has said, "Blessed are those who mourn for they shall be comforted." The comfort comes from knowing in the heart that all is ever present as conscious awareness inclusive of the awareness I am and the awareness that I saw as a loved one. This is the divine unity, the place of perfect balance in which birth and death are one.

Unless I am aware of the immense and immeasurable wonder of the conscious awareness I AM, and even if surrounded by loving friends and having great riches, I might be prone to loneliness and yearning. Under any circumstances, it is easy to be inundated by our worldly conditioning and be plunged into despair, grief, or unwanted emptiness. But if one can bring oneself to see the impossibility of separation from the wonder of all-inclusive consciousness, all problems vanish. Remember, there would be no shadow if there were not light. Consciousness is light, and the very awareness of it dispels shadows.

More simply, perhaps, is to see that even as I am writing in a journal about some misery and unhappiness experienced, there would be no light on the page or pen in hand unless conscious awareness is ever present permitting the Is-ness of it. This very seeing is itself the healer. Said another way, because God is all as awareness, where is there that to be healed?

I will answer that. As long as there is a sense of a separate me, there is plenty to heal. Not so long ago, I was also deeply immersed in the darkness of a me-sense. As painful and unhappy as I found it, and dearly as I longed and struggled to escape it, the old habits of thought persisted. Not until I gave up the struggle and surrendered the desire to escape did the first glimmers of light begin to appear.

Believe me, I understand how real the illusion of the me-sense can appear, but I give thanks for every evil day of it for goading this man on and on until, exhausted, I gave up. It was then that I discovered the imbalance in me that was the cause of blindness. At the center point of balance, the view is total and all the battling opposites are equalized.

As one emerges from the darkness of a me-sense, the world appears far more wonderful and full of light. It is as if one had not ever really seen it before. One discovers a new happiness that leans on nothing but the very joy of being aware. Life loves those who love life. That love is not a possessing love or a hanging on to life fearfully, it is the loving wonder of the awareness you are.

The stone and the hand

As I sit and listen, I hear the immensity of expressions that encompasses the entire universe. The universe is discovered to be here within and not out there at all. The stone appears to be out there, so appears the boulder and the mountain, and so do the Moon and the astronaut playing on its dusty surface.

But where are they really? Right here. They are always here as this very conscious awareness that reads these words.

We project our world and give it weights, textures, and history. We say this stone consists of a particular arrangement of atoms, even as this hand that holds it also is an arrangement of atoms with age, history, and change. We might examine the stone with the same curiosity with which a brain is examined, but most of us fail to see the wonder that is both the stone and the man examining it, as is the Moon and the astronaut.

Most lookers are conditioned to the idea that all things are separate, distanced, spaced. But if stone and man lie not within the awareness man is, then where else can they possibly be? All right, the man viewing ceases to be a man as appearance. Does this mean that the identity of stone and viewer all disappear? To human eyes, yes, but all that is as conscious awareness remains as principle— Godhead. Let it all cease, yet pebble, boulder, mountain, and all the rest, inclusive of the identity we are, remain forever within conscious awareness, or Godhead.

The stone is a marvel even as the body of man is a marvel. The stone is a galaxy of atoms. The body of man is a galaxy of atoms. As stone and body, each is a galaxy of atoms differently arranged, but of the same original energy—Light. We may hold the stone in hand, even as the boulder holds us seated upon it, and stone, boulder, and man are all supported by mountain. Experience kinship with all that exists and you shall never be lonely.

As human appearances, we pass in and out of levels of sense and the understanding of it. The pebble on the beach or in the garden is relative to the Source even as we are. Perhaps the words I write make all this complicated and involved, but essentially it is the simplest and most wonderful experience of unity with everything as One, which we call God. At this point, all questions and answers fade away and in their place is the ineffable, unspeakable being. May I share the joy of it, the stone and I?

This morning in the deep stillness of 3 a.m., the eye was seeing the hand as an extraordinary piece of machinery under the guidance of, and obedient to, the something that ordered it—the super wonder. It was seeing that one must not stop at the image of flesh, but go on through, deep, deep, and behold an image that can be experienced but not described. For seeing it, really seeing it with the inner eye, I want to go to the rooftop and bellow out for awakening. The wonder! It is music beyond music, song beyond song, this wonder of wonders, this love beyond love.

The question has been asked, "How do I find what you have found?" In return, I ask, what is it you are looking for or expecting? You will not find it in any mental concept of things; therefore, stop trying, stop looking in the wrong direction.

Stop all looking based on inside-outside or good-evil; stop looking at opposites. Stop all that and be as still as the stone appears to be. In this stopped state, see what is still and always present. It is conscious awareness. Keep looking at this wonder until you see that there are not two, the looker and the object, but one only, a wonder you cannot find words to describe. Let it be so. It is nothing but your belief in a separate me-thing that blocks the understanding and experience of that which is the real presence of almighty being—God.

When all that is perishable and passing is gone, where are we? Keep asking, and keep looking where no in or out is. Find the place of perfect balance. It is a divine place, and you shall have discovered what emperors would give an empire to discover and be.

Limitless love

Love. Such a much misused, abused, and little-understood word. For most, it is attachment to this or that image or to a sensation. Can I write the true meaning of love? No, I cannot, any more than I can describe what the principle of conscious awareness is or what God is. We can be it. Love is what we are.

I can tell you what it is not. Love is not about an image, and it is not an object of desire. It is something greater, much more than big or little and more lightful than light. I might say it is the fire of life, but what is that? So, the heart sings its love, and in stillness, it can be heard—a wordless song, soundless sound, ever awesome, ever amazing.

True love is like the sun star. It cannot be made to shine here or there as a person might wish. It shines equally on all alike. Where love is concerned, there are no limits. Open the heart wide. Let it be filled with love and give without stint to all regardless of appearance or the rubbish that might issue from the mouth. Love transforms both the giver and the receiver.

Let the light felt in the heart shine forth equally and freely. Love such as this transforms the world. It cannot be willed, fashioned, or made from plans. This world is full of magic. The impossible is ever possible.

Love already is as the heart of one. Let it take over, ending doubt about direction or action. As spontaneity, love knows exactly the right word for the moment and the right way to proceed. Give wholly all you are to God and see.

Immediacy of Truth

The immediacy of Truth bypasses any thinking about it. All mental considerations are secondary, and if this is understood, nothing can be added from the intellectual level that will bring Truth and the wonder of it any closer than it already is. Is it so difficult to see that the infinite cannot be brought down to finiteness without losing it and leaving only an image or a symbol of the original?

Instancy has no past or future, but past and future are contained within it. If we stop to look, it is not there. Consciously to be the conscious awareness that we are, to live the wonder of it, is the point of this experience on planet Earth. It is to delight in it, celebrate it, love it.

We as human beings are here for the discovery of, and the conscious being of, God's wonder that we call awareness. We are to discover the perfect guide within. It is the Christ Child, the true Self of every one of us, the everlasting spirit that is the guide.

There are moments of wordless happiness that defy any mode of expression. There is an all-thoroughness, a gift without equal, a place where words stop. Seeking outwardly or from a mental conditioning is where a veil seems to fall, and the pain of believing in loss drives us again to seek a way out. Thus, we become like dogs chasing their tails, going around and around in circles seeking that which we are. And what are we really? We are that very Christ Child that is within us.

There is Light that is greater than light of sun or lamp. It moves not. It is still and immense beyond measure—Father, Son (Child), and the spirit (the reality we are) all as One. Here is peace beyond the understanding of peace. There is power both omni-latent and omni-being as one infinite, glorious, motionless center. Here we are close, and the closeness fills the heart with a joy never known before.

No one can explain why he or she loves. Without love, life seems to be a living death. With it is life, real life, a life of freedom and happiness that no man-made law can shape, increase, or lessen. Unplanned and unbound by human ideas of limits, Love is. Love has no equal or master save God.

What relation has immediacy to Love? Love is spontaneous, immediate. Where can a line be drawn between immediacy and Love? Are they not the same? True Love, love without object, without desire is ever present; it does not come or go. Earthly life as bodies appears to come and go, but Life and Love are eternal qualities of almighty Being.

It really matters not what is written or spoken. To hear and experience this infinitely immense wonder called conscious awareness seems to absorb all and reduce mental effort to nothingness. What is truly wonderful is that the person-me-thing simply disappears as if it never was. There is no room for it: Is-ness fills every corner of the mind with wonder.

The human mind struggles to find phrases it considers sufficient for the expression of truth. All the while, wordless, soundless wonder is going on infinitely beyond any possibility of language to express. Be still, listen; be and give praise.

Another world

As the years roll along, another world becomes even more real. The old, familiar three-dimensional world grows less and less important. With a widened awareness comes happiness without cause—and less and less ability to define it.

As I draw closer to a magical threshold of another dimension, I wonder if an old ant might experience such change as he becomes aware of a once unknown three-dimensioned world, the one which for us is so familiar? Questions, questions, yes, but all the same, there is an assurance that is unexplainable and lovely.

When my sister was seven years old and I was six, we had a nurse who told us about a huge bearded man called God who lived up in the sky. He saw and knew everything and had our names in his great book. When, before bedtime, we said our taught prayer beginning with "Our Father," we saw a bearded old man scowling down on us. It was a scary image.

Now, going on 92, when I say "Our Father," there is no old man. I am held, inundated by an awesome presence that is everywhere and everything, and it is not scary at all. The presence is so vast and sweet and infinitely lovely that wording about it simply comes to an end. But, at last, I am really living. The human person is a servant, no longer a master. Hallelujah and amen!

A visitor asks, "How long do these wordless places last?" I ask you, how can such questions be answered? I know not, for where the new dimension is, time as we know it ceases. What can I do? What can I say? I find nothing satisfies the yearning for some way in which to acknowledge the Love that I experience. Is there any way to describe such profoundness? I find the search for words is fruitless, a waste of effort. The singing and pure enjoyment in the heart is not expressed for sight of eye or hearing of ear. If you come to visit, all you see and hear is an old man growing older, yet he is a Child. He is free. He says, "Happiness is my way."

I cannot trust knowledge. I am nearer when I admit I know nothing, and I just be this wonder called conscious life. Now "I" am this wonder, am fulfilled, am assured, am happy beyond cause. I have discovered that if I let go of my ideas of how and when, and just listen where there is no sound, I am shown without a doubt the way to go or what to do. It looks like magic; it is the magic that happens when I get out of the way.

Do you need a name? Then go ahead, call it God, but don't see a white bearded old man scowling down at you through the blue sky.

Lifted up into the new

It is perhaps one of the most wonderful experiences in life, this honest waiting to be lifted up into the new. It is a state of nearness to the discovery of a love that loves the ignorant, the disloyal, and the self-idolaters equally as the saints and the devoted true. It is the discovery that true love does not discriminate, does not judge, does not have preferences for this or that. It can love beauty with the same verve and understanding as non-beauty. Images or appearances no longer are a concern. The wonder that is life, the consciousness that is awareness, these are the wonders.

So few seem to see anything of the actual being in which they live and have their existence, yet that sight is present. It is ever open, and the only shroud that hides it is the personal sense of man.

The question arises then, what is this that I am? It is the asking of this basic question that begins the journey of discovery up the mythical mountain. Only through persistence in asking does the marvel of being reveal itself. Only little by little does truth reveal itself.

I have been asking the questions who, why, and what for many years, and today, I experience an ever-growing closeness to the wonder that is both the one who experiences and that which is experienced as one. I can more and more live this that is and be the link with the unspeakable that is conscious awareness.

Stay with the turmoil. Live it and understand it. I see no help in retiring from this scene to convent, monastery, or ashram. There is no special place for enlightenment. It is always with you.

Releasing your hold on life

Awareness of your heart's truth arrives little by little as on silent feet. It might be unknown to the busy mortal mind that does its chores and cares for the needs of its body, but heart's truth is not found in thought about it or in holy books, manuscripts, or letters.

In utter stillness, it holds you as if the arms of a loved one are around you, and a knowing of oneness precedes all else. You no longer react to irritants of any conditioned nature. Thus, there is serenity and no effort to appear as this or that. Discovering this Being and loving the wonder incomparable is all that's needed, nothing else.

It happened to me one evening on an October 9th. Simply put, I saw! Nothing was seen with these eyes, but I saw! I put hands to head and bent down in awe. I cannot word it, but it happened right here. I was in a kind of shock, yet in glory, and the heart sang. It could be misleading even to mention it. The man who sees can never be the same again. The glimpse awes, and there is rejoicing; yet the tongue is tied. What took place has in a way blown person apart as in a great wind.

What happened has no dimension as time or place. It was sudden revealment. No revealment of any kind can happen with mental effort. It is in the state of no wish, no plan, no word. It is to have no hold on anything, and such a state cannot be contrived. It happens. It happens when one gets out of the way.

This is true in relation to any action. I know if I put out the water-colors, brushes, and paper and tell myself, "Now, I am going to paint," then nothing happens. Or, if something appears, it is a mess, a nothing.

A friend who lives here is a real artist. She told me she never knows when inspiration will come upon her. She never has anything ready. Once, she told me, she was on her way to a luncheon date, when she turned back and fled to her studio. She forgot about the date and painted all afternoon. The result was one of her best works, which was purchased by the Brooklyn Museum. It was a wonderful confirmation of being in a state of no hold on anything, only letting be.

Also, an actor friend once told me that if he thinks he is acting a part, then he's dead. "I relax and let the role take me over. It's the only way."

Life is full of opportunities to prove the value of letting go our hold on it. Let us ask ourselves, do we really have faith in the wonder that made us? Can we let it be and not interfere? That is the glorious proof.

The place where "I" stops

At this moment, what am I to do? Where are the words that can express what is in the heart? Inspiration has no outlet, and I am used to having an outlet. All I can do is ask for help and wait.

How does one get lost in the maze of mental stagnation? It is like a dark forest, but I know it has a purpose or I wouldn't be experiencing it. I must find that purpose, and if I understand the purpose, I will discover the path that leads into the Light.

The heart yearns for Light. It loves Light. How shall I find that path, Father?

I sat in the darkness and waited. Faintly, at first, I heard it. I listened intently. There came a feeling that I already knew the answer. I, as conscious awareness, . . . Ah, yes. When conscious awareness stops being of planetary origin, then the wonder is experienced and Love is unveiled.

How do I know this? It must be the experience of timeless wonder right now. It is as if there were nothing but ocean and I am in it at last. I was always in it, but I believed I was only the river that went winding in and out, seeking a way to that ocean.

Understanding that the ocean is ever present and that it is the only real presence brings the end of negation, worry, and fear. It is the place where real living is.

These words are but a faint echo of the experience. I must return to that place where terms stop. Within the place of stopping is the art of turning away from personal sense. Personal sense is like a backwater—it goes nowhere. I must again find the main stream of present wonder.

No form of words can bring about the experience of ever-present wonder. I have heard present wonder termed as "the action of God the Good." If this or any other term sparks a glimpse, then let go of the term and follow the glimpse. To stay with terms is to return to the swamp and go nowhere.

The circuitous river does usually come to the sea where its toil is ended. And so I go on prating in the hope that possibly something written will reveal the joy that has no end. That joy is ever present. Experienced or not, it is always with us. It is simply a matter of loving "the Father" enough to stop in that place where personal sense is relinquished, and where ever-present, timeless joy is experienced.

Breaking through the shell

The only thing to break through is the hard shell of personal sense, which is the conditioned sense in which we struggle, ache, hate, desire, and sometimes kill for what we think we want to acquire or for what we think we want to discard. Whatever it is, it is a confinement, and a loss of knowing what we really are.

That dark, world-made shell is to be broken. This is its purpose. At first, we might make a small hole in the shell through which we receive a glimpse of a wonderful and infinite world of amazement, and it holds the attention enough to keep us pecking away at that shell. The need to get out grows and grows.

Let's shuffle the old wording to see if we can develop a new expression of being. We are finished with the old shell and all the familiar ways of words. Oh, there will still be words; you can count on that, but listen, we can step through the familiar phrases and discover there is no law that says it must be said this way or that way.

Listen again, let's clear our minds of the acquired learning, things read and heard. Let's forget all that and see what life is like for the new one, the one who has not yet heard or seen a word. Behold the wonders of the infinite variations of light.

See that wonder we now call a tree. See it without the label. See that wonder of flight known as a bird. All is fascinating wonderment; this thing I grasp, the feel of it, the look, the scent, the taste, unknown as sense, but it all is related to a special wonder we now call consciousness.

That which we see is all-surrounding. It is a peerless companion, an ineffableness of light that is both light and shadow and that is the very one who sees, a something of endless horizons where the sounds of voice, wind, bird-song, or the jingle of glass or metal are all tones of a symphony, mysterious and lovely.

As this unnamed something, you are really living, and though you have never heard of God's universe, you are truly enjoying it. You can enjoy it now, again as you once did. Yes, you can. It is here, the same as it was then—all light and wonder. You can be it and you can live it—your very real self. Remember, where words fail, living takes over.

Happiness without cause

What amazes is the number of these so-called years that have passed without any understanding at all of the marvel going on. Now that it enwraps and is so tremendously present every moment, I wonder how the distractions of the conditioned mind could ever have been great enough to screen the wonder that was missed. I confess it did, and those years were sad and sick.

Has anyone yet discovered what Love is? Maybe we have been living it. But can you tell what it is? I am sure you cannot, not any more than I can tell you what happiness without cause is. Asking what is causeless love or causeless happiness is like asking how the cell was invented or how gravity was invented. I do not hear the scientific society offering answers yet.

But after all talk and thought, which serves to distract, is let go, I am unexplainably happy. The aches, pains, drought, frost, dead trees are present all right as all appearances are and are prone to change, but appearances they still are. Nothing changes the unexplainable wonders of being. Thinking about it, or imaging about it, obscures the scene.

No matter how sure we might be that we are alone, we are never alone. That which formed us, grew us is ever present. How do I know this? I cannot explain. We have not yet discovered any way to express the infinite in finite terms, but I have—and I'm sure you have—experienced in a glimpse the wonder of Being, which cannot be proved any more than we can prove what causeless love or causeless happiness is. When we feel lost, deserted, isn't it the personal sense of us that has pulled us down into the dark? Mortal appearances deceive us into believing we are victims of age, fear, disease, violence, poverty, and so on. All of these establish the

reality of causeless love and causeless happiness. This is the equation at work, the perfect balance in effect.

These are so many words, and they might be read over a thousand times, but they will never produce the kind of happiness I question. I wish there were another expression because the word happiness might be confused with personal or conditioned ideas concerning what happiness is. As long as we cling to a form of any kind, or are fearful for it, or are afraid of losing it, we are caught in the trap of happiness's opposites. While in the trap, it is unlikely we will experience happiness.

Real happiness is the state of being where all holds are let go, all wishes and wants and struggles are erased. And if this sounds like a definition, it is simply my failure to say it correctly.

The other day I asked a visitor to tell me what color is. She responded, "White light broken up into its components." All right then, I asked her what she saw as light. "Light comes from our sun." Ah yes, and where does our sun come from? She hesitated, and then said, "It's part of God's universe, isn't it?" And what do you see as God's universe? She thought for a moment, and then asked, "Why are you doing this to me? I'm no scientist."

Right. And I am not one either, but if a scientist is asked questions until he comes to a stop and says, "Oh, so you're one of those metaphysical nuts," then you will know that he is refusing to tell you the simple truth that there is nothing but conscious awareness, and as far as we can possibly now know, there never was anything but conscious awareness.

I am fully aware that all of this is naught but repetition. How many ways are there to say the same thing? Yes, a limited number. Anything composed of words is limited, but when we are still and are listening to nothing, thinking nothing, just being, then wonders do happen to us. We do not want for proof because we are what we experience. Thus, I admit I have come around Robin Hood's barn in trying to express what real happiness is or what love without any object is.

Why try? It isn't anything any of us can get or apply to ourselves. We already are it. It just needs uncovering. It is here and now, and let's give thanks for it.

Release

Here on planet Earth, I sit with a journal on the knee making endless scratchings, not merely in reverse of doing nothing, but to ease the heart's deep wish to express an overwhelming love, of something truly nameless that has to do with the wonder of being aware. The pen hovers in the grip of helpless inadequacy. Now look at what is scrawled in the journal, "If there is a way to prove this sweet wonder that invades, I pray to be shown the way."

Yes, I have been praying thus timelessly. I have discovered that the way never appears as planned, never as hoped for, or in any appearance of mental imaging. The way appears, unprepared for and unexpectedly in an unlocked moment, and it amazes as if a veil lifts off the eyes. Why, it is right here. It has always been so. I have always been on the way to discovery, so have you.

For years, I was blind and unaware, sure, but there never was anything else. The way is what I am, what you are. Do I know what this consciousness is that I call fact? No, I do not. I live it or it lives as I, but no one honestly knows more than that. However, as I become more and more aware of being this wonder, I find I live in what I call the sweet nearness.

Perhaps to the young, old age looks pretty grim, but let me tell it. For this ancient one, this is the happiest, most beautiful time of a long life. How come? The appearances are that I have less freedom, less motion, less of everything, including hair and shape, but these are the lesser blessings. There are blessings today that were never dreamed of.

I see how commonly everything is taken for granted. For so many years, I lived the daily actions never looking or really seeing what this living was, never questioning these appearances. I was content to put names on everything and to dismiss them without any understanding. I was like the blind man with his hand on the tail of an elephant and saying, "Yes, this is a rope."

It is so easy to put names on everything, to dismiss them as such, and to never see anything. On the walk here is a common dandelion that is standing straight out of its phalanx of serrated leaves, a golden orb of many tiny flowers. But it is not common at all. It is extraordinary, a form of life.

But what is life, really? Where did it come from? A seed. All right, tell me about the very first seed. You smile and say nothing. Don't worry, the question is never answered.

It is true we too are mystery even as is the dandelion. The scientist tells me all about the seed and the cell, the black hole, the nova, gravity. He is full of names, but I still know nothing beyond limited sense and guesswork. Why is there such resistance to admitting that I know not? I am here. I know that all right. Great, let's go with the one fact we know: conscious awareness is. This is the wonder.

If I let go of mental pondering and agree to be as still as that dandelion, something within begins to sing. It takes over and erases that puzzling me sense. I am lifted up into a wonder of happiness.

If you want a name for it call it pure being, but the moment you try to name it so that the conditioned human mentality can catalog it, you have lost the incredible understanding. The more that conditioned thinker tries to hold on, the less he has.

It has been a seemingly long road for this one to learn to let go, not only to agree to be the empty cup, but also to agree that nothing of the world is mine—never was. And now I give daily thanks for that long and tortuous road that is leading home.

Home to the boundless sea

What makes a man so sure that he knows what is what? When he looks outward and beholds what he calls his world, what makes him so sure he is truly seeing it?

Begin with the room here, the walls, the windows, the furnishings. The body can come in hard contact with one of these, and the hurting member knows about so-called matter and pain. In this way, beliefs are formed. But does the man stop a moment to ask what is behind these appearances, experiences, and beliefs about them?

If he stops for a moment, he might say that the world he sees, including his body, is prone to destruction and that all might vanish at any moment. But does he ask if anything is imperishable?

As a child, I was thrust into a world of sense, where pain and pleasure seemed to go hand in hand, and I began to forget the pure state of being. I was wound about by a new world of sense—a place of discovery and of short-lived happiness. I found that life is like the waves of great rapids on a river, up here and down there. I found that most of us are tossed about like chips of wood or are swirled into a backwater where we go around and around, getting nowhere.

I was thrust into that backwater by a big dose of personal sense, and I went around and around in that backwater until the yearning to be free grew greater than any sensual experience could ever satisfy.

Eventually, I was weary and disgusted with the burden of hells and heavens of a personal sense world. I prayed. I asked, "Isn't there anything imperishable in this experience called life?"

It was at this point of asking that the first glimpse of the pure and unchangeable fact of consciousness was itself seen as imperishable and indestructible. I was amazed that I could have lived so long and not have seen the wonder called consciousness, the very conscious awareness I was. "Why, consciousness is the very essence of the whole scene! I am living in wonder and as wonder, and I never knew it! Consciousness must be in some way the very action of something vastly real and indestructible. Dear God, that changes everything I ever believed and thought."

It is a confounding realization, and yet something within is singing and full of joy. Wonder on wonder! Here is the place for anyone of us to end that bumpy ride down the rapids and float out into the wide calm of the river. Here is peace unlike any peace ever known. All tension is gone as one floats easily on the way home to the boundless sea.

Yes, I am still in the same old room full of familiar things. I still inhabit the same old body. What then has changed? The importance of everything has changed. I find I can let go of things and beliefs easier. I can let be. This is the beginning of true freedom, of spontaneous living.

I find my association with others changes too. I am now the helper, not the judger. If rapids appear in the river of my life, I ride them without fear. I am the master, not the victim.

Once, I might have believed I loved, but now love has naught to do with appearance, sex, or attitude. It goes far deeper, and those once passed by, now become the friends who are in need of help. With joy I am that helper. As joy, I live. It makes all the difference.

Meditation

Why have I never spoken of meditation in any book or letters? This question was asked by a friend. In a way, it came as a surprise. For a moment, it was incredible to me that I had not actually written something what is to me the whole fabric of living.

Perhaps I have avoided using the term meditation because it has become so involved with the lotus position, the body just so, the breathing this way, the hands and fingers that way, and so on. I must have taken for granted that readers had also discovered that the very awareness of being is meditation no matter what position the body might be in at any particular moment.

The questioner went on asking, "Isn't it necessary to set aside a particular time each day for emptying the human mind to be still and listen?" Then, I understood that the friend was speaking from the point of view of a person involved with worldly business.

As my friend insisted that time should be set apart for quietude and giving attention wholly to awareness of the wonder we call life, his words brought me a smile. I saw no argument at all. Basically we were in total agreement.

But I had discovered there is no effort at all in what is referred to as meditation, no working in the head. It is simply a matter of letting go of everything, inclusive of any mental image of what constitutes meditation. If one is saying, "Now I am meditating." Forget it. Such is not meditation. If I know that this awareness I am is not mine, but rather an action of the ineffable wonder, it is easy to get out of the way and be in close relationship at any or every timeless moment.

How sweet this thunderous silence, this infinite stillness that erases the learned, personal mind of man and leaves one vulnerable to un-imaged, living God! When we make the imaged world out there and the imaged world in here as one, then we have discovered "the Kingdom of Heaven" and we are that "Kingdom."

I see that this is a new day, one never before experienced by any living thing. But I also see that this is the same continuity as ever was. I wonder if continuity smiles at the divisions into days, months, and years in which the life of man is involved? Being, the "Father" that created all living form, is continuous; therefore, awareness, the action of the creator, is also a continuous activity.

Call it meditation if you want, but I see that the prime discovery is infinitely simpler than I once dared to guess. No wonder this amazement leads to much troubling of the personal sense mind. Do I hear a voice crying out, "Dear Lord, how could I have been so blind as not to see this continuous wonder that awareness is?"

Oh yes, it is wonderful, unspeakably wonderful to be aware of this tremendous being. Now, I let go of all the wonderful teaching that prepared me for this moment. I let go of everything once considered holy and necessary. It is a joy at last to be personally nothing. I keep nothing, not one single belief in this way or that way. I am nothing but an invisible, silent wonder found deep within being. It changes one to understand that this view is the treasure.

It becomes clear that the human sense of things as out there and in here and all the habit thinking deeply darkens the view and for many appears impenetrable. It is not impenetrable. Living, and all its experience, sooner or later drives us out of the darkness into the understanding that we are truly an unnamed something that is beyond becoming and beyond perishing.

Blindness

The other morn the light on the foothills and the granite peak beyond was extraordinary. There was an incandescent look to the scene, and above the mountains was a flotilla of white clouds like great schooners in full sail driven by a fresh breeze. I had to share the feeling the scene gave me, especially so because I knew the scene wasn't out there but right here as the awareness I am. Therefore, I could carry it intact.

Back in the building, I sought Helen, the tiny lady with the wispy blond hair and shining sightless eyes. I found her sitting alone on the lanai. I came up behind her chair, and before I reached her, she called out, "Good morning, David." How she knows the presence of her friends before they announce it, I don't know. It is her secret.

I took Helen's outstretched little hand in mine, and as best I could, I described the scene planted as awareness that morning. There is a light that illumines Helen's face, which is far more difficult to describe than the light on the hills that morning. Sharing any eye-seeing with this lady is for thin-skinned David an emotional experience.

Later, as I was leaving Helen, Evelyn came along and put her arm through mine. "Tell me, David, what is it you see in that wizened little face that makes you weep?" I had to say something. I told her I must be getting senile. She laughed and let the question about Helen go. How could I have explained? But I did ask in silence, "Who now is the blind one?"

Incredible wonder

A friend reads the pages of the newsletter and discovers typos and extra punctuation floating about. Today, this friend asked, "Don't you usually send four or more pages? There are only two here." I sensed that only the number of pages was behind the question.

I told her I recalled a time in my own experience when I had a large bookcase stuffed with hundreds of books, thousands of pages on the subject, but at that time I had no real understanding.

Later, I discovered one could go all over the world listening to gurus in ashrams and never get beyond a personal self stuffed with metaphysics.

Then from whence comes understanding? Of course, each finds it exactly at the right moment and in his or her special way. And I doubt that any of us can compress into words that wonder moment.

I recall a visitor once asking if I didn't find life in a single room among a conglomerate of rooms a lonely affair for an aging person. I knew he was seeing an ancient man gazing out a window, but that appearance is a fragile and misleading one. I laughed at the question. Sadly, the visitor did not see the happiest of creatures who was unbound by four walls or creaking joints.

How does one tell it? When I look out that window, I am not seeing out there. I am here within and I am part of an incredible wonder going on. I am free, freer than that bird. In the identical moment, I am in Love and as Love.
For many years of living, I was a prisoner within the shadow of a dream of a personal sense, and the deeper and more painful the

shadow, the closer I came to understanding and release into Light. I wonder if the joy of such release can be expressed.

It is neither lovely feelings nor ugly feelings. There is no good day or bad day. It is ever the wonder of being this awareness. No good, no evil, no saint, no sinner, no youth or old man. Then what is it? It has to be something. Ah yes, so it is—this very something consciousness is. Isn't it wonderful?

Happiness

Today, I walked the paths about this place where, because of a prolonged drought, the eye was aware of much sickness among the plants. Yet, in spite of this, I found unexplainable happiness neither within nor without but here and everywhere.

I cannot tell you what in this world I have to be happy about. You would see an ancient man more or less physically restricted in a place of retirement for old people. He walks with a cane. He lives in one room. So, you might wonder what there is to make him happy.

I cannot tell you; yet, the fact is I am happier than ever before in a long life. Some might say age has made a simpleton out of me. Yet again, I tell you I am as healthy in wits as ever.

How then can I explain or share? The answer is, one has to discover true happiness for oneself. I have found it; therefore, anyone can. Happiness is right here closer than close, right where you are and as you are. Perhaps that is why it is so difficult for many to discover. It is overlooked.

I am like a man in love, one who has found the true love of his life. The beauty of it is that it does not ever change, age, or grow familiar. It is ever a mystery, an extraordinary wonder. I go to sleep with it. I awaken with it. I am with it every moment of the day and night. I revel in it and am as if intoxicated with the rich wine of belonging. That which reads, creates, is awareness, and much, much more is the wonder I love.

Just being

I was telling a friend the other day that every morn before breakfast, every evening before going to bed, and sometimes in the middle of the night I sit here on this straight chair with the journal on the knee. It appears to be a habit, but it isn't. It is always new, and it is wonderful. How can I express it when it seems to be nothing? Ah, but it is tremendous, just being. There might be writing and there might not be. It makes no difference.

You know all the terms, such as stillness in which the physical man, the personal sense man, is as if dead. You have read all the words about meditation. "Be still and know." But do you know the wordless state I am trying to express? Do you know the state of simply being what is? Are you engulfed as in an infinite ocean? And at the identical moment are you that ocean? Do you experience something far beyond words, a happiness and completeness that laughs at any attempt to express it?

Ah, then you do not have to read these words at all. We can stop and go out and play or stay in and play. We can look at roses, watch birds, hear the sounds of life all around us, and of course, we can do all this without moving at all if that's the way it is.

What a vast difference there is between reading and thinking on these things and actually being them. We can bridge that chasm in a great flash of lightful understanding.

Now, what do we do with it? Ha! Nothing! That's the beauty of it. Nothing to do, nothing to say, no one to convince, nothing to change, and nothing so great as letting everything be the way it is.

Real freedom

Living the balance between getting and giving is where real freedom is found. Few, if any of us, have even touched the hem of freedom as it really is—freedom from conditioning, freedom from the old family backgrounds, the induced or inherited likes and dislikes of this and that which created the personal sense we live.

But that personal sense can be used for the glory of God. That personal sense can be taught, and it can be trained to help us discover the wonder and the awareness we really are. Trapped in this personal sense, any glimpse of hell can delineate the glory of heaven. Being awake to that glimpse can show us a world we have never seen before, and we can experience what is meant by being reborn.

The entrenched me-conditioning is the only devil there is, the only Satan. It whispers depressing, disturbing thoughts. It tempts with thoughts and emotions of spite, retaliation, jealousy, hate, violence, all untruths, and the most vicious of all, ennui. All forms of blindness to what is real lead to misery and defeat, sickness and death.

Are we free to choose our way? Yes, we are. Nothing is standing over us ordering or commanding us to live as unhappy prisoners of personal sense. It is we alone through our conditioning and acceptance of the personal sense as real that makes us prisoners.

All things are possible to those of us who have awakened from the dream of me and its personal beliefs. In that knowledge, we are free to choose the way of peace and causeless happiness, a way in which we serve our others instead of self. We can thus become a light in the murky darknesses in man's world.

As dreamers, we live chained to patterns established by our surroundings and those with whom we associate. Most of us strongly resist all attempts that threaten those patterns. We cling to the established, whether we call it modern or ancient, and believe we are right. The belief that we are right is dead and stony ground. Through doubts in the pattern of living and through the discovery of the power of love comes the ability to cast off the chains and be free again as the unadulterated Child.

There is no command for anyone to remain prisoner and victim of a background and its beliefs. Dare to look honestly at moment-by-moment living and really see how we got to be this or that kind of man or woman.

Through this seeing, the chains that have held us down so long are cast off, and we are truly reborn as new.

Mystery and wonder

You can stand on the shore and watch the water as a wave breaks over pebbles and sand, but you cannot say you know the ocean. If you cross it in a sloop, can you say you know it? Its width and depth at every point? And even if you are an oceanographer, your knowledge is based on limited human sight.

If I ask you what is life, you might point to this creature or that, this plant or that. You can dissect, photograph, x-ray it, but you'll never tell me what it is. I'm not asking about shape or blood or bone or muscle; I'm asking you to tell me what Life is, its awareness that moves it. Not the cleverest physicist, the brightest scientist can tell what Life is.

I can say only that I know life as I am being it. That is such an infinitely small knowing, like a drop out of the ocean. Taking that drop to the laboratory and determining it is a lot of chemicals does not say what it really is. Names, weights, chemicals are only substitute terms for not knowing. So, we live in and as mystery. We are the mystery—the wonder.

It's easy to say, "Yes, that is so." But do you experience the mystery, the wonder? Do you feel the presence of the unknowable in your heart of hearts? If not, you are missing Life all together—missing awareness, God's presence, God's plan, God's love.

May you see the wonder that you are.

Find your own way

Writers tell about their way, but it's necessary to find your own road. I crossed this continent many times by car in the old days before freeways and pikes made it easy. There were no maps of the open roads. There were three known routes: the northern route, the central route (66), and the southern route (89) through Texas.

Sometimes there were long detours because of floods, repair work, snows, and so on. You found your own way. Sometimes the roads were paved and sometimes they were not. And when not, they were dusty or muddy or full of holes. You never traveled without chains, shovel, tow cable, and emergency supplies. You found your best way.

The southern route was the first to boast pavement all the way from coast to coast. But that was not to be relied on because that pavement might be under four feet of water or in repair. The detours were pure adventure.

The only route to true life is the one you hack out for yourself. Oh, the pointers and experiences of others are helpful, but in the end, you have to find your own way. You might think you are paving it to make it easier for others, but each will go the route that suits his individual needs.

The route you carve out for yourself is the one that gets you there. Along your way, you will make new discoveries and see new sights.

On the coast-to-coast runs, someone would ask, "How long did it take you?" "Oh, I made it in six days." Nowadays people drive night and day and do it in three days or less on freeways, or they fly it five hours. There is no feat to it anymore.

Such is never true of the routes to self-realization and true living. There are no freeways, no airlines, no train tracks, and no fancy strip maps—nothing to make it easy. Yes, many accounts of writers are helpful, but there comes the place where the books are put down and you actually start out on your own.

You will never build a house or bake a cake from reading a book of directions. You have to do it. You will improve your skill by making and correcting mistakes. You will create your own recipes to fit your own needs and taste. The house is for you to live in; the cake is for you to eat.

You create your own routes by doing not by reading. It is your work that is of value to you not someone else's work. Get in there and find your route to true life.

Part 3

Excerpts from the journals

God and Is-ness

Do I know what God is? Beyond such words as universal energy, unconditional love, and love unqualified, what does anyone know? The human mentality knows nothing. It can conjecture until it is worn out, but it will never come near the truth.

Something is indefinable within us that simply knows, without any proof or argument that the Power is here as all. It roars like the surf. It sings like the lark. It shines like the sun. It rushes seaward like the mountain stream. It is the sprout of grain that grows and grows and blooms and seeds. It is the rose and the thorn tree. It is as the sand, the rock, and the cloud. It is the nearest and the farthest star. It is. It is! This I know!

Is-ness does not come and go. Is-ness—God—Spirit—Source is ever here and now. Any appearance to the contrary is illusion. A man might be the image of goodness or the image of badness in the world, but images are illusion. All man is one.

Is-ness precludes is-not-ness. Any darkness, sickness, violence—any imperfection—seen in the world results from a belief in something less than almighty Being. As long as man, immersed in his belief of twoness, remains divorced in his awareness from the one I AM, then man sees a world of anguish.
It is all shadow. To be aware of the nonsubstance of shadow estab-

lishes a constant knowing that lifts awareness above the shadow world. The ever-present I AM is the light that discloses the living Presence and eliminates shadow.

Be open to the enormity of Is-ness. True listening is a state of complete surrender and openness to God, or whatever term one uses. It is a state of grace, and only in a state of grace are we ready to receive enlightenment. Whether we are on the Tao way, the Zen way, the Theosophical way matters not. All ways are spokes of the same wheel.

Another way is the way of the heart, which is instinctual, unique. It is the way of truly seeing oneself, listening and waiting in readiness. This vulnerable state has not been taught or acquired in any way. It is recognized through a feeling of rightness and harmony. Trust it; rely on it. Go to the center within you to know the power of humility, the power of joy and pure love. Here, there is no objective but to be.

When you ask, "How may I behold this I AM? How do I find it? How do I make it real?" The answer is, it is everywhere. Everything you see and all you never see is this I AM. It is the entire reality of you. You cannot grasp it anymore than you can grasp the infinitude of Is-ness, yet it is ever closer to you than any person, closer than that "me" you believe is something. I AM is the only reality. When you understand this and become one with this understanding as your daily life, then the change appears. Then there is transcendence, and then you are above all worldly things.

The fruits of your experiences in time are the learning of and the knowing of I AM. If this were not so, there would be no purpose to limited, dimensional experience. Nothing that is of God is without purpose. I AM has its identity—an everlasting identity—in limitless Spirit.

To be constantly aware of the one reality of I AM is to be at peace and to experience the joy, wonder, and delight of ineffable Love. The more this union with I AM is experienced, the more it does not matter that it cannot be explained in human terms.

Awareness of God in action is the most wonderful, actual, real experience of life. It is life. The Is-ness of God is more real than any belief or concept man ever made. The awareness of the Is-ness of God is unspeakable joy, where all things are possible.

When the world seems to invade and separate one from the peace and surety of wholeness, where politics, division, and threats of violence seem to leave one stranded, there is a way to return to tranquility.

It is in watching the brain imagery until it slows and finally hides from the Light turned upon it. Now, the curtain of thought and personal sense draws back to reveal the quietude of vastness beyond measure.

This immensity called consciousness is ever present as the Presence that surrounds man's petty otherness and drowns the ego with an infinite ocean of purity in its tremendous Is-ness. This all-encompassing wonder is the wholeness that heals and erases the little cares of man as if they never were.

□□□□□□□

Divested of all imagery and religious symbolism, the essentiality of God is free of all human mystique. This fact of conscious awareness here and now is seen not as something added to or separate from life but rather is its very existence every moment in every breath.

□□□□□□□

Jesus is a manifestation of the Christ as a man. The Christ is ever Spirit and is here abiding in the heart of all men whether seen or unseen. It is the awakened ones who feel the living Christ within as love transcendent here and now.

□□□□□□□

The power of the Christ within is wholeness. Wholeness is the totality of all facets of God. Be aware of the total presence of God everywhere, in everyone, in every thing. It is a special blessing to live and understand the infinite immensity of this wonder of being we call God. There is nothing outside this that we are.

□□□□□□□

Nothing is outside or separate. God is not a once-a-week something to confess to and get pardon from. God is omnipresent, eternally being all we are. Every breath and heartbeat is God functioning as a fact of life. Life as wholeness is eternally going on. Births and deaths are facets of this functioning. God-Life is eternal, and this is what we are right here and now—eternal divinity, eternal Being!

□□□□□□□

To experience God's eternal presence is to dispel all shadows so that we can see clearly what is going on rather than what the conditioned self thinks about it. Clarity of vision turns the seeming dark to beautiful Light.

□□□□□□□

When I come before my Lord, I admit I know nothing. I come empty, waiting to be filled. This feeling of being empty of all knowledge, all images, all sham, all ego desires is a necessary state of humility to be in if there is to be a feeling of joy and ineffable Love. I am freest when free of every term and phrase and word of man. Thus, empty of all pros and cons, I am a singing child standing in the Light.

□□□□□□□

To love God, we are to be free of personal thoughts and free of all desire for personal results.

□□□□□□□

Our habit from an early age is to put God somewhere else, any-where but right here. Source is not apart from the I AM that we are. God is the only reality there is.

□□□□□□□

To the man whose eye is single on God, there is nothing that is not God.

□□□□□□□

A god that is created in thought and image dies when attention is not on it. Such a god is not absolute or ultimate but only a figment of the human mind. That which is, the true God, cannot be contained in human concept or circumscribed by human thought. Yet, it is eternally present everywhere as all.

□□□□□□□

God, the Is-ness of all, is now and only now. Now is the only point where true Being is—all else is folly of separate thinking. I exist only as this eternal and infinite moment—right now. Right now is heaven. Right now is help, is inspiration, is supply.

□□□□□□□

Evil is not real. If it were real, God would not be an omnipresent God. If God created evil, God would not be a god of Love. No, evil is a creation of man. Man creates evil through his inattention to God. All the world's problems are the result of man's fragmented attention. With man's attention fixed on the wonder of Being, the world is paradise.

□□□□□□□

Many talk a lot about God versus the devil. There is no such God and no such devil. There are no opposites of truth. Truth is wholeness. The only God is without opposites. The only God is oneness as all. The only devil is man's ignorance, his belief in dualities. The only devil is man's nonunderstanding and his ego.

This blindness appears to work what we call evil. It is all based on illusion. He destroys nothing but himself. God being one sees no duality. Dual belief is illusion. Only one wholeness as the principle of consciousness is real.

□□□□□□□

Freedom is so close you cannot see it. It is seeing God as all, as perfect and omnipresent. The unity of wholeness cannot be diminished. It is so simple there is nothing to write. One can only repeat the one truth in infinite ways. Nothing is going on except God being God, Is-ness being Is-ness.

If you are alive and conscious, you are in the presence of God. If you despise your world and yourself, you despise God.

When you are aware of wonder, when you love the wonder, when you turn your eyes and thoughts to the wonder, all else is added in such a rain of bounty that you can never want again. You have found God. You have revealed the hidden one. You are in the constant presence of the Source. Then, the wonder is all you are.

All philosophies are spokes of the same wheel. There is nothing to fight about or feel separate about. We are all one in God's view, Allah's view, Buddha's view. To fight with each other over terms and prayer habits or organizations simply indicates a gross ignorance. We all have this in common: I exist. I AM. Consciousness is, and that's what I AM.

There is no other, no god placed apart as something for which one stops living to go to some other place away from the here and now. To see this is a revelation—to be so keenly aware of the Presence as all here and now. It instantly changes life to see God as present in every movement, every moment of being alive. To see this does away with other forever.

The Light and you are one. The Being and you are one. The leaf, insect, cow, cloud, hill, ocean, the moon and sun—the universe!—are one. Praying becomes a present conversation of sharing. Putting God away as something outside of you separates you. There is no other.

The one who has surrendered all to God is not moved by what the senses react to. This is why the man of God is ever at peace and is tranquil no matter what appearances are. He fears nothing because he is constantly aware of his union with Source. The most deeply ingrained habits of thinking and reacting fall before awareness of the single and only presence of unnamable Source. To know life is to shed every last shred of personal and separate belief and to give all that is real back to unnamable Source.

The Father and I are One is surely the essence of all the revealments made by the Master Jesus. Keeping this focus is the answer to all appearing human problems. Awareness of this divine unity lifts man to the heights and returns man to the God energy. As this union, man is changed from the sufferer of effect or karma to the pure freedom of the angel—the servant of God. Recognizing the truth of divine union changes man from the victim of effect to the freed Son of God.

I live not my life but the life of God as this consciousness I AM. I no longer have to go anywhere—to a church, or temple, or meeting place. I am surrounded wherever I am and am ever in the temple of almighty Being.

□□□□□□□

God is closer than breath, waiting recognition.

□□□□□□□

Give yourself to God every morning and continue to do so all day. Your life will be lifted up. Try it before you doubt it. Give one day— all of it—and see.

□□□□□□□

Conscious awareness

You have two wills: the personal and conscious awareness. If you let personal will fall away, you are automatically reunited with God's will as conscious awareness. This is where you are at peace beyond worldly peace. This is entering the Kingdom of Heaven.

Awareness is the great gateway, the portal of wonders. It can only be approached by stilling thought, which is entwined with worldly conditioning. Only when the labyrinth of concept and belief is still may one enter the holy place of union with Source. The only truly positive reality comes to the open heart not through the brain.

Learning to see the wonder Source as conscious awareness, the magic point, within you performs miracles of healing and changes the course of life. It is the healing point, the place of miracles, where you move from the shadow to the Light.

Keep your full attention on conscious awareness. Just begin, and once begun, your ability will grow stronger and stronger if practiced many times a day. See the wonder of your existence, the principle of conscious awareness. Here is where you rest on the wonder point where no personal sense is, only the love that directs you to the center of wholeness and tranquility.

However, if this exercise of attention becomes rote, a system, and if the exercise itself is taken for the point, you are then in the same old box of personal business as before and no magic is there at all. Set aside this personal syndrome and be open, vulnerable, and in a state of waiting. It should be as natural as breath. Let the heart's need to hear and to feel the presence of almighty Being be the focus.

The glory is all around us. The human state is essential for seeing this as the great opportunity for mankind to discover the fourth dimension of consciousness and to live in it and be it. Where truth is realized, there is always a confirmation, a surge of love response in the heart. This is the guide.

The breakthrough into the unlimited dimension of Light is not reserved only for the vigorous. None are so weak who cannot be aware of the conscious wonder we are and then follow consciousness as it grows toward its infinite and eternal source. Attention on consciousness every moment of the day is where the power is and where the joy of living is.

We can entertain only one attention at any moment. If attention is on the wonder of infinite awareness, it cannot also be involved with human problems. Here is bliss, where the secrets of the infinite are revealed. There are no bounds to what can be attained; it is only a fixed belief in human limitation that has kept us from the fruition of breakthrough into infinite realms of conscious awareness.

So many see Spirit, God, Perfection, Divine Love, and so on as something to get or achieve when Spirit, God, or whatever term is used is always right here as the conscious awareness we are. Spirit is to be realized not achieved. What already is, is to be experienced where it is. There is no travel to be done to find God. No one can endow you with what you already are endowed. God can be revealed to you as being the essence of you as it always is, was, and will be. It is this that so many do not seem to realize. All is here right now. It is a matter of discovering it as already yours.

Life is incomplete without awareness that is free of all consideration, of honing, of pruning, of paring, and free of diminishment or of adding to. Allow it to be itself. Let there be no imprint or image there on. Let it be clear, open. Let it be void of all ego. Let it be like the wind where there is no human alteration of nature. Let it be like the unseen and unknown. Such awareness knows no qualifications whatever but is as uninterrupted pure Light. This is the Light that the heart seeks through the haze and murk of dualistic thinking. This is the true nature of all. This is the home of I AM.

In union, in oneness, there is wholeness; there is perfection. No matter how the senses insist on discomfort, keep the attention fixed on the all-inclusive, ever-lasting presence. This does not deny the senses; it does not claim that the senses do not exist. Rather, recognize that what the senses insist on is separation.

Evidence of this separation is seen through wishful denial. It is not healing or wholeness to simply relegate one interpretation to outer darkness and seek another interpretation in its place. It is to abandon all interpretation, both supposed bad and supposed good, and realize there exists only one reality, which is the inclusion of all. There is no outside.

Do not resist the unwanted, but seek to know its purpose. Lift it up as an offering to union ineffable. Return to simple, direct knowing. Stop struggling, and open your eyes to the wisdom that is all about you.

It is the very simplicity of the secret of eternal life that escapes mankind. Those who have any care at all in this direction look to a long and difficult road of study, of gurus, teachers, and intellectual accomplishment. They look to physical exercises, tricks, and so on to bring them to nirvana. This is all the personal sense way and brings one back to where one started.

The true way is awareness that I AM exists. The awareness that comes from knowing is itself paradise won. No man can teach another the recognition that awareness is all. He can only point the way. It is each of us who makes this divine discovery that is our being, our true nature, our sonship—that which we already are.

Forget the vulnerable, passing, and temporary, and look to the real, eternal Being that is awareness. Hang on to nothing: not the body, not the body's senses. You have an awareness body that is not victim to thought appearances or sense beliefs. It is the eternal body. Go naked to God with nothing but awareness itself. There is no mind, no life apart from God's awareness and that awareness is I AM.

The blessing is that one can be and is aware of the Light even though it cannot be distilled to a finite distinction. It is still recognized by the luster it leaves on the page, on canvass, or in the sound of many instruments. It is also glimpsed in the eyes of a friend and in the beauty where no duality is.

And where does one find such beauty? In and as the conscious awareness one is, where all opposites are made one. The eye of flesh sees the fallen flower, the bloom, and the bud. It sees blight as well as beauty, but true eternal beauty is the love in the heart of man that knows no opposites. It views the fallen flower, the bud, and the bloom all as part of a whole where the beauty is. It sees destruction and creation as one divine principle expressing as a three-dimensioned appearance. It is in the whole view that true beauty is.

The common term here is known in relation to a geographic spot. But the term also denotes the mystery of Being regardless of place. Each of us is ever here right where we are, and this here-ness has nothing to do with place. Such here-ness is the assertion of consciousness itself. I exist here, never there. Consciousness as divine here-ness is placeless and timeless. This now-ness is infinite. To give whole attention to the infinite, eternal moment right here, right now is to face the wonder life is.

We call things ordinary that we see everyday; yet, we really have not seen anything at all. We mistake familiarity with ordinariness. When we really see principle in action as conscious awareness, we see nothing ordinary–all is full of wonder and joy and mystery.

Everywhere is a holy place. Right here where we ever are is the place of worship. The man, or woman, or child next to you is a bearer of the Divine One, the Light that is conscious awareness.

□□□□□□□

The aware one is reborn every day. When free of conditioning, the mind of man opens to new dimensions of thought and greater awareness that is unlimited by the world's logic or reason. Awareness includes much more than a visual, audible world. Free of all suppositional barriers, the aware one beholds a new universe, a new language free of senses.

□□□□□□□

We never get out of personal darkness by studying the darkness. The fascination of its habit is the temptation (if you like) of the devil. The only devil is the darkness of ignorance seated in personal sense of separation that the individual accepts as real and which is not. There is only one reality, and it is the very fact of our being, the very fact of awareness. There is nothing else to be.

□□□□□□□

Prayer is not something I have to speak or write; it as the sky and the sea: always present. This prayer I know is awareness. It is consciousness of being. Where least expected, it is clearest and strongest. Blessed awareness is not a prayer for something to be, it is glorying in the present wonder of being.

□□□□□□□

The man of senses is nothing and can do nothing himself. Experiencing God as the consciousness that I am is the only power here present, the only doer. Such realization is to be deeply imbued with the action called life, or God action, and is to be seen and known through the only one to whom all things are possible. Only when there is a ceasing of thinking and appearing as man and transcendence of what the world calls mankind is the spirit reunited.

Although the day is nearing an end, there is no end to conscious awareness. A life seems to wane, appears to come to an end, but there is no end to conscious awareness. No end, no beginning—always here, always being that which it is: the endless mystery of life as I AM.

Consciousness does not die. Consciousness—the I factor—is an attribute of God; therefore, it is eternal. What is there to fear? Nothing real is ever lost. Much that is believed to be real is lost. Life is an attribute of God and is indestructible.

How can the temptation to look back into a dead past be cured? Many know that looking back is the cause of depression, regret, and dissatisfaction. The important thing is to be aware. If you are aware that you are looking back at "better days," days of cleaner air, quieter life, of personalities, of events, then you can see the waste of energy it is.

These are the days, not then. Now is the time, not "when." This is the moment divine. Here is where life is, not in the mistakes, laughs, or pain of the past. Now is the harvest. Life is now. Walk out of the shadow. Behold the living Spirit. Seek the companionship of the soul. Seek the companion presence of God in whom consciousness is merged.

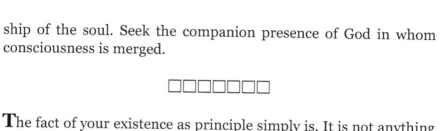

The fact of your existence as principle simply is. It is not anything made by man and it is not possible for man to destroy it. In death, your appearance—your body—may cease to function, but your consciousness does not cease to exist. The principle of consciousness never was that appearance, any more than the sun is the patch of light that shines through your window. That patch of light moves about and disappears, but the sun has not disappeared.

Hereness can be as small and cramped or as tremendous and free as we would build it. We settle for the awareness we live in. If we make it small and cramped, we are ever subject to boredom, loneliness, and sameness.

God knows I might spend many lives thusly, but one day I discover I need not be cramped by little emotions, little desires, and little ideas. I can soar in every direction at once. I can be an infinite universe so beautiful, so full of marvels that I can never describe it.

One often hears the question, how can God permit such suffering and evil on earth? As for suffering and evil, ask man about it. They are man's problems; he is responsible. From man's ignorance of God, he accepts the appearance that God causes suffering and evil. Do not blame the One for man's blindness. It is up to man to return to the sonship he is. Know that you are a form of conscious awareness, which is the wonder of God on earth.

□□□□□□□

You live in an ocean of almighty Being. There is nothing else. What your eyes see or your senses feel is but a facet of the gem. Look to the core of the awareness you are. If you are missing this, then you are asleep in a dream. Awake!

□□□□□□□

The presence of God is in every moment. Past and future are ideas of the human time sense. Be rid of this time limitation and see and hear beyond eyes and ears. The wonder is right now and you are as the Presence.

□□□□□□□

The light that transforms what was once seen as ordinary into such beauty and newness and wonder is the Light of awareness. Wherever these eyes look, the reflections of this wonder are awesome, and the beauty is beyond telling. This tree, which I see every day, is such a symbol of glowing Love that the eyes of flesh falter, but the eye of the heart is filled with wonder.

□□□□□□□

Seeing has nothing to do with eyes. Seeing is an interior event.

□□□□□□□

Mind

Clear the mind of all that you know is not God. Examine every image, every thought. Discard any thoughts that are not God. Attend to this with deliberate intent and see that the more that is cleared away, the lighter and freer you are.

As you proceed, you see that all these images are tainted with the limitation of worldly conditions. Not one is worthy of standing before the Light, the Love you feel. Let the emptiness be filled with the Light in place of all that once busy thinking. Now you see what you really are. Ah, so you are amazed. You find liberation; you are silenced, awed by something beyond telling, something ineffable.

We don't realize the power of thought and what we are continually doing to our lives and bodies through the power of thought—misguided, conditioned thought. The destroyer of joy is the belief in a past and future; it is the thinking that indulges in memory or fear of future, and so loses the reality of the Kingdom of Heaven here and now.

It is possible to raise thought deliberately up and away from all worldly considerations. It can be observed rising up and away. To know there is no limit is a tremendous in its realization. This is part of what is meant by taking command. It begins with command over thought because within the conditioning of thought begins all that is not the Self.

As you raise awareness higher and away from an ego-centralized level that possesses a kind of mesmeric enchantment, you are magically freed from both lower-level pleasure and from its opposite, misery. In the rarified atmosphere of awareness freed from worldly considerations and beliefs, you come to that which you truly are: Spirit not matter. The experience of being one's true and free nature is being what life really is—pure enjoyment, dominion, wholeness.

Meditation is the purity of being that is free from all time and memory mirages and can be understood only when the mind and its décor of memory is stilled. Simply, it is keeping attention focused on Is-ness, this wonder that we are. It is listening through, seeing through the curtain of human beliefs and thoughts to this ever-present reality.

When the human mind is filled with its own places and images, it is missing the wonder that is here and now. Let life be spontaneous, aware, and loving. I AM is all peoples, all colors, all beliefs. I AM is all life, great and small. I AM is all that is made and all that makes. I AM is the beginning and the end as one.

A mind unencumbered by conditioned memory is not a mindless mind; it is simply a mind free of concocted belief and personal memory. It is still mind, still aware and clearly seeing Is-ness rather than the parade of well-known thought all based in a worldly view. This mind has pure awareness untainted by personal history, desires, opinions, or beliefs. Total oneness, which is pure awareness or God, means no personal mind with its memory is possible. To understand this is to live in the only real moment—now.

Freeing the mind is rebirth. Keeping attention fixed on this open, alert mind brings forth automatically the health, happiness, and tranquility we seek, as it fills the body with Light.

The secret is not in thinking but in listening. Still the thinker.

How do you expect to realize the one perfect Mind as the awareness you are if you are forever listening to your own voice, either talking to others or to yourself? This that talks and talks and conceptualizes and imagines conversations is the blinder that shuts you off from what is real and what is really going on.

Be as still as you can, no matter what life demands of you. Let it unfold as it will, but you remain like the eye of the storm, always calm and serene in the realization of pristine Mind, pristine conscious being—the source of all and as all.

For the greatest joy of being, turn away from all programming and see that the once faraway God is right here, closer than any worldly

parent or loved one. It is pure happiness to be free at last and ready for the greatest adventure of all.

After all the years of having your thinking guided by man, held within his limited world of social mores, and trapped by the world's accepted patterns, consider now turning away from all those believed-in concepts. Consider now opening the forbidden door of the mind to an infinity of being. Consider now going through that once-believed solid wall of reason and logic to let go of all conceits. Consider now going beyond the pale shadow of the real to see everything as it is. Now see through eyes of I AM, which is the true nature of all.

Nothing can be done to stop the activity of the mind. Its function is to be active. However, what is controllable is the subject or concern of the thought. When the thought is permitted to run on of itself, it disturbs, worries, indulges in dreams, and it can destroy you.

You do not have to surfer from a wild, uncontrolled thought machine. You can say what the quality of thought is that you live with. If there appears a dragon, something undone that you would rather not do, then clear it from plaguing thought by slaying the dragon, by doing that which must be done.

The mind is a great instrument, and it is to be trained to do the bidding of the immortal I. The power of the thinker if unleashed is a destroyer of all around it as well as itself. Channel this power to carry you forward into the new dimensions that are here all around you ready for discovery. The first step is to be the master of your thought. Let it be directed and tamed until it is completely docile and obedient to the transcendent I of I AM.

□□□□□□□

The invasion of the mind of mortality, the programmed mind of beliefs, of long habits, is the nearest and most familiar enemy. It is of no reality; yet, its seeming reality is so strong, most of us cannot escape its clutches.

Imagine being a slave to a myth-like mortal enemy. Yet, there is a nonfailing defense that few know of. Employ the real watcher and let it be the guardian of thought. Let it watch over all the ghost-thoughts that have surrounded you, that have become the personal you.

I AM immediately brings order and peace to chaos. The watcher simply watches the mind of mortality and scatters its unreal forces. Be free of this nearest enemy and have freedom from all mortality.

□□□□□□□

Struggle and mental effort only make life miserable. Be quiet; be still. Listen for inspiration, and forget appearance. Do not try to alter a thing by your thoughts. The human can do nothing of itself. Turn away from the body and its desires and rest in eternal Spirit.

□□□□□□□

The dramatizer of ideas by thought replaces action with a dream or vision based on desire. This is an evil practice for it is an inversion of the energies given to man. This misdirection of ideas turns in on man to destroy peace of mind and heart.

To be free of the dramatizing habit and mind, recognize when you experience the invasion. When you recognize it, know deeply that you do not want this experience. Unwanted and dismissed, these invasions of energy are a bother no more. Turn away immediately from it. Turn to the reality of the consciousness that you are.

One can get lost in an idle mind and wander forever, seeking nothing and finding nothing. The human mind is to be trained and made to work as a means of experiencing what is real and of discovering what is not real. The idle mind is a dangerous mind—disorderly, careless, vengeful, self-persecuting, and a slave to judgment and opinion. Gently guide the mind with love and kindness and it will answer every wish.

We hear a lot of talk about junk food, but junk thought is more prevalent. Junk thought is aimless, tiresome, uses energy, and often affects the body to the point of disease. And a large segment of souls limit themselves to being acted upon by junk shadows on a screen. They are adding junk images to junk thought. But once aware that such junk blocks the Light, we can then remove the blockage and behold the Light. It is we who limit the power of awareness; it is we who limit the power of God.

When an unusual occurrence takes place, the conditioned mind immediately searches for some logical explanation for what it is not familiar with. Why can't we accept what is seen by a more sensitive eye than the flesh? It is because we do not yet understand the simple intelligence of a field daisy, which with its bright head of multiple flowers is surrounded by a mandala of pure white petals.

□□□□□□□

Hell is a state of mentality in which the presence of God appears to be absent. Such suffering is an illusion. It is choosing human will and its wants over surrendering to God's will.

□□□□□□□

Well-rested, the human mind is so active that it elbows its way to the fore and blocks the view of infinite wonder. It takes patient seeing of the activity to hold it. Seeing this is the rein. Watch this to still the mind. The watcher is the eternal One. The human, not wishing to be observed by such infinite tranquility, leaves the arena empty of itself and what is left is infinite wonder.

And when the mind is not rested, it is full of its aches, weariness, and self-pity. This also stands as a block unless one is aware of this up and down nonsense. Be aware of the folly, the feeling good and feeling bad. Watch and be free to see what is eternal.

□□□□□□□

The human mind is ever ready to make a disaster out of every appearance in its physical body. It ignores the power of God, which is its life, and creates otherness too easily. The mind misuses its wonder. In harmony with Is-ness, the human mind is a servant of almighty Being.

□□□□□□□

You don't let go of the wheel when you are driving, so why do you surrender your mastery of thought? Isn't it there that tragedy and accidents happen? To conquer the habit of letting the mind drive itself is to enter paradise.

□□□□□□□

How can God speak to your heart when there is such clamor in your mind?

□□□□□□□

Make the leap from the conditioned personal mind to the freedom of silent perception and understanding. How beautiful stillness is. It cleanses the body and mind. The mind is free to see itself, to see its tricks, habits of thoughts, and its possessions. Only through recognition and understanding are you freed from the dream state of the human. Only then are you ready to enter the no-world of reality.

□□□□□□□

The battle with the human mind is not necessary. Simply turn away and see the wonder that Life is. Battling only strengthens the foe and wears you down. It is difficult, if not impossible, for the human mind to understand anything where there is no object and no concept of an object. If your attention is held only on this void, chances are you will discover—to your amazement—the truth.

□□□□□□□

The Self

All knowledge, all wisdom is where the Self is; therefore, there is nothing to learn because all is. "Learning" is for the belief in a separate being looking to attain something more than already is. The Self is the wholeness, the true nature of all beings. See no shadow of separation; there is but One, and this One is Love, and Love is I AM.

No one can give us the secret of our reality. It is an open secret. It is hidden because we are divided and looking everywhere and see-ing nothing. No one can convince another of the joy of being whole. No one can describe it, paint it, compose it, dance it, or in anyway pass it on. It is here within us. To be aware of it changes us, to be it changes the world.

Being is not something you find outside of yourself. Come out of your separate idea of me and be amazed. The wonder of life unseen for so long confused with science and medicine has ever been here all around you. Eternity is now. Freedom is now. Perfection is now. God as I AM is here and now.

It is difficult for a programmed humanity to understand what is neither visible nor touchable. But the Self cannot be described, inscribed, or circumscribed. The Self is what you are after the fire has consumed all visible signs of a body. The Self is beyond being destroyed or created. The ray is to the sun as the Self is to God. The Self is the radiant energy of God experienced. Know the Self through perfect stillness of unconditioned thought. As such stillness, nothing is left but awareness itself.

Does a rose give a sermon on how to be a rose? Your true nature cannot be found by struggling because it is ever-present. Your true nature cannot be acquired because it already is, was, and ever shall be. If you try to grasp it, it will elude you. But still desire, thought, and speculation about it, and you will see the wonder it is. Once beheld, you are reborn into a true state of being.

Personal senses, being illusionary, cannot possibly affect in the slightest the constancy of that which is. Do not be misled by the belief in senses that might give the impression or create the mirage of less or more realization of that reality. Once released from personal sense impressions, suggestions, or mirages, then you behold the true nature of Is-ness. To be free of all such conditioning brings the realization and experience of almighty being.

There is nothing to struggle against; nothing to strive for. This is so difficult for man to understand. Although he might not yet be aware of it, his total perfection and oneness with the Father are already established. This cannot be changed regardless of his human shortcomings, his crimes against himself and others, his worldly record. No matter how absent this perfection appears to be in the life he is now leading, it is present. But he shall be reborn and reborn until the perfection he is unfolds and is made evident in its glory.

The body is believed to have a life of its own, but it does not. It depends on the health of the psyche or soul, and this in turn is directly affected by thought, attitude, understanding, or the lack of these. Good health or wholeness depends then on the state of mind. If the mind is full of anger, fears, judgments, ego concerns, and so on, then if it is not evidencing ill health, it is certainly building up to it.

Heal the psyche first and the body will respond. To heal the psyche, move thought away from past and present into now, this wondrous moment of all Being.

The mortal person really loves all the sad drama of grief and pity. It thrives on this destructive emotion. It clutches onto every prop and suggestion of loneliness. This is of absolutely no value to life. It is the destroyer of peace and quiet; it is the destroyer of Life's true nature, which is to be joyful and to rejoice in the majesty and wonder of this creation. Be mindful of the ever-lasting I and touch the Spirit that is I AM.

The nature of God is known to the Self. The core reality of man is the spark of God that is the awareness of I AM. Knowing that there is nothing in the universe other than the power that conceived it propels one beyond the belief in sickness, pain, or lack.

□□□□□□□

By your fears, you are the judge of how far off center you are. Examine the fears in your humanity. Ask that there be freedom from humanity and from all illusions. Let go of the imaged world. How can the life of man unfold if he is ever in the way, blocking the Light with his image constructions?

Only your soul, your true nature and identity, can tell you when you are on the right path to useful creation. Perfect harmony is experienced in continual confirmation. When such harmony is missing, retract, reconsider, and begin again.

□□□□□□□

Be aware of perfection ever present and let it guide you. Your body functions perfectly in response to the law that created it.

□□□□□□□

We tend to confuse the bodies we live in here with eternal qualities. The body of flesh belongs to Earth, but the awareness that inhabits it is the evidence of eternal power.

□□□□□□□

As the "me" belief diminishes, there is less resistance to living as wholeness, to not be limited by old background beliefs. Breaking down all old resistances is a joyfulness to the soul. You can be anything—anything that is necessary at any time needed. It is replac-

ing cannot with can that evidences wholeness. God puts no restrictions on I AM.

□□□□□□□

To be united with the soul, one is to be totally at peace. This cannot be if a human wish, a human will, or a human image or concept is in the way. Let all go. Ignore appearance, claims, and all familiar beliefs. Once having transcended the human image, one is free.

□□□□□□□

Contentment is not dependent upon conditions of earthly origin. Contentment is free of all likes and dislikes and has nothing to do with vicissitudes. Contentment is an awareness of eternal qualities not temporal moods. The one who seeks it in worldly conditions will never find it, yet it is always closer than one's very breath.

□□□□□□□

Light does not reflect until something is put in the path of its flowing energy. When you can be open enough and clear enough of me-sense, then you reflect the Light. This is individual and solitary work, but the individual outcome benefits all.

□□□□□□□

The Self knows no opposites. The Self is calm and unmoved by the shadow show. That which roars and weeps is not the Self but is fragile and temporary, an appearance. The Self knows neither depreciation nor inflation. The Self is constant, all-loving, all-powerful being.

□□□□□□□

Instead of resisting the wind, I am the wind.

□□□□□□□

It is a common mistake to ever look outward for answers when the magical secret is within us.

□□□□□□□

No matter how far one appears to have strayed into a self-made darkness, the way back is ever open to the true nature of one's aware Self.

□□□□□□□

Beliefs

We are free to take dominion over beliefs right now. Patterns can be changed; we can change ourselves through being aware of pre-programmed thought patterns. We can refuse to recognize them. We can turn away from old beliefs and stop creating new ones. We can be as free as is our true nature, our real and eternal self. Consciousness is the only reality. What kind of world we build out of it depends on the degree of limitation we accept.

Do you have a lot of beliefs? Get rid of them, if you dare. It takes courage to face life without beliefs. When all your beliefs are gone, what do you have? Trust. That's all. Trust in the heart, a surety that has no proof, no logic, no reason. People say you are mad. Most of the world can't live without its beliefs. They say beliefs make a man sane.

Then let us be mad. As we let love take the place of beliefs, then we are open and vulnerable, but we are also fearless. The Wonder of Being rushes in and awareness takes over to reveal the marvel of existence.

Often it is our beliefs and our fractional lives that appear as barriers to purposeful action and tranquility. We hypnotize ourselves into not being able to do this or that. The dropping of both beliefs of "I can't" and "I can" solves the problem. One who cries "I can" and "I will" is admitting there is "I can't" and "I won't." When the two opposites are dissolved in wholeness, there is doing and being.

□□□□□□□

That world out there that you despair of is the result of the kind of thinking we are all guilty of. There can be no change in the world until everyone individually sees the truth within. We must turn away from conditioning to see what we are—to see the real power and the pure love we are. As each of us transforms, the world is transformed. The light we shed will have a positive effect on all with whom we come in contact. All we can do is change ourselves.

□□□□□□□

Everyone must eventually face the concepts and beliefs put upon us. We have to be free of all that before we can possibly know Truth. We have to step out alone and find what is for ourselves. No one can tell us or make us believe. We have to relinquish all the memories of what the world has accepted and strike out naked and unafraid into the unknown. Let God find us in God's own way.

□□□□□□□

You are forever seeking within concepts, and this is why all you ever find are more concepts.

□□□□□□□

Those who chose to live in the shadow should not complain of the dark.

□□□□□□□

What good are the religions of the world if they keep us separated and hating each other?

□□□□□□□

The Lord's Day is not always Sunday. It is any day when there is recognition in full of the absolute being that is God—the I AM.

□□□□□□□

Beginners tend to separate their devotional life from everyday living, but as they grow in understanding, they see there is no division. The divisions are a human idea and not true. As separation disappears, daily living is the devotional life. It is all the same. Constant awareness of the presence of Wonder cannot be relegated to a special time of day or night. Seeing this makes every moment of awareness holy.

□□□□□□□

Come up and away from the conditioned thinker, the man of mortality and past errors. Pay no honor to the images, to the twisted memories of foolish days—not even the honor of being thought of. Turn back to this moment and the awareness of Being that is real and perfect. When you are still and experience the healing love flowing into your awareness, open the doors of the heart and let it pour out to the sick and fearing world.

□□□□□□□

The divisions in your life, all the events and fears and beliefs that you hold separate from God, are what cause all your troubles. It is the sure knowing of the Oneness of all as God that heals. As long as you hold on to this or that and claim that it certainly is not God, then there will be the trouble, pain, and disease that the separate idea breeds.

Confess to the almighty Being all your secretly held fears and guilt beliefs. Letting go of them is your cure, your peace of mind, your way to salvation. Bring these errors into the Light of truth and repudiate them. See them as lies. Call them by their names, and command them to return to the nothingness from which they appeared.

When you believe there is someone or something other than the one and only mind that is God's awareness, then you complain of being shut out. You feel isolated and miserable. It is only a belief, and it can be eliminated through understanding the truth: No real mind is in operation other than the one mind that is God's awareness, God's consciousness. Anything that can be eliminated, that can change, is not real. Conscious awareness is real. Let this reality shine on you, and stand in the light of it.

We see what we deem as unjust, terrible, ugly, and depressing. We ask how can God express such a world? God does not express such a world. It is only man's limited belief in interpretation through personal sense that sees the illusion and believes it to be real. Man through his ignorance makes the hell he sees and experiences.

There is no good versus evil; there is no "versus" anything. To call God good and man evil is the dual illusion of man and God. Only when the two are understood as One is the Kingdom of Heaven realized as it is—without all human qualities and judgments.

□□□□□□□

A prison built of belief has no locks or bars, yet it is still a prison. When you are busy looking back, looking forward, dramatizing, making thought-movies, or in any way using the energy present for amusement or indulgence, then awareness of omnipresence is blocked. You cannot serve two and be one.

□□□□□□□

If you are doing anything about enlightenment, stop! If you are thinking anything about enlightenment, stop! Stop it all, and be.

□□□□□□□

As long as you think of enlightenment as something to be obtained, you will never come to enlightenment. When you understand this, you are enlightened. You understand this when you see that there is nothing to get.

□□□□□□□

Life is not a whim or an accident of conditions. Awareness, not memory, is the mysterious wonder in which we have our being. Contact with Presence cannot be broken. Neither sin nor death can break it. As living creatures, we are already irrevocably united as one with Is-ness.

□□□□□□□

Suppose you never heard the word God or Christ or Law or any metaphysical terms? How could you express your feelings? Removing all the metaphysical terms produces a special quiet. Absence of words does not diminish happiness; rather, it increases it. Find what is in your heart and let it come forth undiluted. Then, the body seems to lack dimension. You are a free-flowing response like a river. You are no longer bound in a dimensioned course; you are a river without banks.

All is part of this something we call God. Consciousness is as much a facet of God as the eye or ear is of this body. There is no outside, no place other to be. Come and see the omnipresent wonder we are. Study no system. Let the way appear naturally as it is. There is no how-to or when-to. We already are. All it takes is an honest prayer from the heart, asking to be open and free.

We don't have to retire to a monastery or a secluded place to discover the alchemy of life. It is present in the humblest actions every moment of every day.

Our educated tendency is to limit ourselves in all our doings as human beings, but if we see ourselves as something more than a limited person-ego, then all limitations fall. As a human, it is well to agree that as egos we of ourselves can do nothing. But as we rise from the me dream and are open to infinite energy, infinite power, then things we couldn't possibly do previously become not only possible but done.

Inspiration is a natural state. Enlightenment is a natural state. The darkness of human concepts that reacts to every physical change is the unnatural state. Eden is a natural state of mind that cannot be put together synthetically. No lasting substitute exists for the genuine. By our habitual beliefs, we have lost our original simplicity and have lost the true way in which things work for us instead of seemingly against us.

We make ourselves miserable through a belief in time, suffering through longing, loneliness, jealousy, or any other sense. We decide exactly how happy or unhappy we are. We look back unnecessarily at scenes past that make us sad or guilty because we are lusting after temporary things. All the while, we are missing the great gifts that are here for us.

Healing is the recognition of nothing existing other than the pure perfection that is God. Man's belief in otherness keeps him slave to human ills and limited conditions. It is the human dream, the shadow show, the fixed idea that must go. Revelation is like a soiled curtain rising in the mind to reveal what is so and all that is. This frees the heart and soul and opens every door to ever-present Love.

There is no sin in man but what he thinks there is. Tucked away and buried deep within his store of thoughts and beliefs are distorting programs that mar the pure perfection of his Being. In the center of man is the ever living I AM that is untouched by the countless errors of man's thoughts. This is the very Is-ness of the soul. Listen to its soundless words. Let all belief in sin and fault faint away for lack of thinking on it. Life is radiant and rife with wonders yet to be disclosed.

Appearances

Appearances are part of the dream of mortality. The spirit that is the life of us all is forever perfect. We have to live as the immortals we are and not go on believing that there are two states: one of mortality and one of spirit. The two are to be seen as one. Appearances are only effect and never cause. We are to see beyond the mirage to what is real, whole, and everlasting.

Why do so many admit that through God all things are possible yet they exclude themselves from such possibility? The realization of perfection as the allness of almighty Being reveals that nothing exists that is not already perfect. The appearance of imperfection, which is human separateness from the infinite, is merely the challenge to see aright.

Clearing an attachment to any imperfection takes moment-by-moment awareness. Omnipresent prayer is the constant recognition of Is-ness. This state of constant prayer brings healing.

Let the light that is pure consciousness shine into the deepest depths. When the surrender to the Christ you are is fulfilled in totality, then there is no appearance of imperfection—for there was never any separation, never any imperfection.

When the Self, that which I truly am, is defrocked of every old image of what past conditioning thinks I am, or acts as it believes I am, then an entirely new entity emerges unburdened by a single degree of conceit, opinion, reference, or fixed judgment. This is what being reborn means. It is the discovery of the real Self, the eternal one, of infinite being.

This is not possible through struggling to be it. It is achieved through a day-by-day canceling of all old habits and world-formed patterns to dare to change, to dare to step out in harmony with that which appears.

Go with what is; do not struggle against it. Be bold, not from desire or preplanning but by letting go of those holds on what is believed to be me, mine, or separate from Is-ness. Be as a traveler in a strange land. All is new, untried, unfamiliar, uncategorized. Know the power that rules, moves the cosmos. Let it be the power that rules and moves the I that I am.

Where there is a definite direction, go and do; don't reason out of it. Don't say, "This does not appear to make sense. It is not done." Let the direction be itself; let it unfold, and watch for the surprise of the new, the magical, and the original.

Look at every thought, image, word—written and spoken—and try to see how much of what you project is not yours at all but something clinging to you like tacks to a magnet.

Be aware of the conditioned person and its various tricks to establish and promote itself and to make its supposed reality secure in your mind. To be aware of this is the gateway to freedom from such an illusion. In countless unsuspected ways, the illusion of the me seeks to impress with drama, emotion, and lies. If the mind is stayed on the constant presence of God, then no illusion is to be seen.

The body is not yours. It is a wonder-image made for you to occupy and learn. It is not a possession of man; it is part of a great design. You have been entrusted to use it for the glory of the Almighty One.

Be free of the me belief and you will be free of all impurities. Then, you see what you truly are. What a blessing to realize after all the church teaching of "poor miserable sinner" that you are of the same substance that caused you to be. Seeing this, you are illumined, you are changed, you are lifted up and filled with immortal Spirit.

No matter the appearance, Is-ness goes on being Is-ness. Heaven goes on being Heaven. Love goes on being Love. Awareness that is Love here and now does not rest. It never fails; it is never absent. It is here at the moment you are open and ready. It is Love beyond any object; it is love freely given, asking nothing, needing nothing, but giving all.

If joy can come one day and be gone the next, it is not joy. A sense of well-being might be mistaken for joy, but joy is the full realization of our true nature, not for an hour or a day but forever. We do not give over our me-ness in part and hold on to a little of it for this fleeting pleasure or that. We give a total gift.

Joy is the music of God—the laughter, the enjoyment of life free of worldly concern. A sense of aloneness is a sense, and if held onto, we have failed to give all to God. Look at this in the Light. Allowing shadows to be where we live is a denial of the glorious Light of God all around. We interpose the shadow. Step out and away. Look up, here now is the companioning Spirit!

Turn more fully to the real and take less heed of the senses and the images that sense imparts to the mind. Here, you near that state of bliss, not as a moment's flash but as a constancy. You must be constantly aware of that to which allegiance and love truly belong.

This practice brings forth the purpose of all occurrences, which are the teachers, the illumination, and the guides. Only with this practice does life of a human type have any real meaning. In awareness and as awareness, you move ever closer to the divine intention. Be a faithful witness and faithful student in this university of God.

Reality knows not what day it is or what year it is. Reality is—it has no divisions; it is all and whole eternally. There is no night there or day there. No such distinctions are there. Distinctions are solely related to life on this planet. To see wholly is to be whole, and it comes forth to one not from any point within the body but as consciousness itself. Consciousness is not located here or there but is allness without boundary. Words cannot contain but a fraction of this wonder.

□□□□□□□

I am not the person I've always thought I was, nor are you the person I have formed images of in thought. None of us are the appearances we see. It's a sham, like the trade rat's nest—a collection of shiny stuff of every kind: A bit of tinsel, a walnut shell, a ribbon, a piece of red paper, a wallet, bright pebbles, bits of cactus. . .all stolen and put on for decoration. And this is also done with concepts, bits of knowledge, data, and sayings. And under all that weight is something not visible to the physical eye: Principle, wonder, something indescribable. . .the real.

□□□□□□□

Only the experience of Principle can see beyond appearances to the real one we are. It is recognition of something beyond appearance that brings the smile of radiance to a face.

□□□□□□□

What appears as a test or nuisance can well be a blessing. Turn away from nothing of this world. Face it and see that what appeared as a dragon in your mind is but a dove. Go out and see. You will find God everywhere.

□□□□□□□

Surrender all problems and know that what is to be done will be done in the easiest and most wonderful way. Do only what is seen to be done at the moment, always in total faith that each moment will reveal the way, the how, and the help needed. The more worries are dropped, the more the wonder is revealed. There is purpose, and it is fulfilled.

□□□□□□□

Another drop in a reservoir might seem to not appreciably add anything or change anything beyond the drop becoming another part of the whole. Such a drop is indistinguishable from any other drop, yet without them, the reservoir would soon cease to be a reservoir. Although a drop might seem insignificant, it is essential to the whole. Ah, little drop, you didn't know you were essential, did you?

The rose has its life of beauty without voice or fuss.

A master walks through illusion as a one walking through a mist. A master knows the way and knows that the mist is a temporary appearance that dissipates under the omniscient light and warmth of Truth.

Prayer

How do I pray? I shut the door on worldly things. I say, I am nothing without the awareness of God being this very life I AM. I ask help in keeping the eye singly on God, for when it waivers, looks back or forward, the heart aches and nothing is done. But when I am aware of the presence of Is-ness as the I AM, there is peace, inspiration, and doing. I pray to know the infinite scope of this I AM. With attention fixed on this infinite awareness, I demonstrate the abundant life that is the Life of I AM, the Son of God.

There is no better prayer than recognition. Recognition as conscious awareness is the silver cord between man and God. Recognition erases the idea of separateness and establishes our unity with Oneness as sons of God. God is known to us through conscious awareness, which is our life, our being, our all. When one says, "I AM," it is recognition of God's presence. This I AM is not the person of senses; it is the eternal reality of God.

There is a quiet place that is not a room, a house, or a garden. It is not a geographical spot at all. Yet, it is only there that the soundless voice is heard. Be still and tranquil, and listen deeply to hear the music of an incomparable song.

The heart is the only interpreter. This heart is not flesh. This heart is wide and deep; it cannot be calculated by man. It is here that dwells the I AM. It is the fountain of love divine. It is the miracle of infinite Being. Out from the center comes all light, comes God. You are that light. The light is the golden ray that caresses the bud to bloom, the seed to fall, the root to find its way, and life continuing on as evidence of I AM.

Darkness sets the heart yearning for the light. When you cannot live in the dark anymore, ask for the light. Where there is an honest call, there is an answer. It might not be instantaneous or dramatic, but look deep to see there is no want, no lack, no dark place. All is light everywhere.

The Christ is within you always. Listen more closely in stillness. Faith is not given or taken away. Return to that place of stillness as often as needed. The answer is ever-present.

Prayers, no matter how fervent, from a "me" to an unknown God are a waste of breath. There is only one prayer of value. It is the recognition that all is already perfect, that you are already well. The only barrier between you and your wellness is this belief that God is somewhere else and is not the very consciousness you are.

As consciousness, all are one. The Love that is the Being of God is omnipresent. Wishes cannot change the truth. Recognize and agree that there is no reality to any belief that something other than God can be. When this agreement is strengthened by utter faith, healing is a fact!

When heart and mind perform as one, the power is complete. When heart and mind are clear of every mortal trace then consciousness is the messenger of God, the channel where miracles take place and healing love shines like the sun. When heart and mind are one, illumination is no longer a dream, and all is understood.

If you know what you want and ask for it, there is always a response. The problem is most of us do not know what we really want. We might think we do, and we say, "If I had this or that or if I were here or there, I'd be happy." But the desires of the personal sense me are not what we really want at all. They have a way of ending, changing, or getting boring. There is only one real need. It is to be totally immersed in pure Love.

God does not speak English—or any other language of this world. All prayers and writings are nothing unless there is feeling. God understands the feeling that is pure Love in the heart, which rises out of stillness. If the words do not carry with them the feeling, the experience of Love, they are so much sound of brass.

The vibrations of the lower animal can be raised up through the spine to the head and beyond as a channel for higher forces and changed to the vibrations of love, healing, bliss, and wholeness. We can practice raising these forces into higher vibrations to no longer be a slave to chance. We have the choice. We have the ability, but it must be used.

The temptation is to sit and suffer and cry for help. It is we who can help by contemplating and visualizing the energies rising in the spirit. Try it, and remember that you are I AM. Remember that your true nature is as God awareness.

Let us use the powers we are given; let us put them into action. Constantly practice stilling the wandering thoughts, and gently bring attention to the One. To live this practice daily is to change the world.

God, I AM! I give thanks for this lovely day. The heart sings songs never heard before. The music here is grander than any music ever heard by human. This awareness of Being is fulfilling beyond all. This day is new; this hereness is new and never occupied before. All is made new. To the limited sight, there is a sameness, but look beyond! Behold this blazing Spirit! Blessed is the new day!

The quiet moment before going to bed could be called a prayer but not in the sense of asking for anything because all is here. Rather, it is a moment for seeing, hearing, and understanding; it is a moment for relinquishing. It is a moment of bliss and of awareness of this tremendous moment.

The most beautiful words in the language are I AM.

Stillness

Listen, not in the way you listen to talk, music, or thunder, but in stillness. Listen in the absence of person-ego, an absence of all conditioned beliefs, an absence even of absence itself. Listen deep within. What you behold will amaze you.

Sit as is natural and easy, or lie flat, or walk. Stillness is an art that has no dependence on the action or inaction of the body. Stillness is a state of mental quietude that invites the wonder that you are to reveal yourself.

The one who wants to know, who wants deeply to understand and to awaken to the experience divine, has only to return to simplicity. It is as simple as breathing. It is not an intellectual goal to be won. It is only a matter of being still, of freeing the mind of all worldly matters.

It is first nature to be still and listen. We do it easily when we are in natural surroundings, such as a beautiful forest. We listen to the birds, the sound of a twig snapping. We listen intently and we learn the serenity of the forest, of the sunrise over a still lake, of the voices in a waterfall. And as we listen, we are aware of the Being that is I AM.

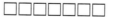

The Light enters when you are still. Push the curtain of personal sense aside and let in that which illumines. Never see the Light as yours; it cannot be claimed. It is the wonder that infuses all who open to it. Call it by any term you want, it is the source of all. Keep your attention true and love that which illumines. Let your life be as spontaneous as the seed that responds to moisture and warmth and good earth.

Stop thinking and listen. Stop talking and listen. Stop believing and listen. Stop hanging on to anything and listen. Be reconciled with everything inside you and outside you. Go out into the world devoid of opinion and judgment. Enjoy the world and let the light of Love shine from your eyes on all alike. There is nothing to fear, nothing to hate. There is purpose in all appearance. Know nothing but the wonder of all life. Revere it. See the Source as all, and sing.

In silence, there is companionship; in talk and dramatization, there is loneliness. In silence, I hear the voice of the Beloved. In silence, I am joyful, ageless, full of awe and wonder. In silence, I see that which is obscured by talk and logic and reasoning. In silence, I am united. In silence, there is no me. In silence, there is Love.

Nothing is so enthralling as deep stillness. Here is the flame within us that ties us to the great mystery of awareness itself.

The peace beyond understanding is the peace of stillness when the busy thought-machine is quiet. Out of this stillness comes all teaching of Truth, comes inspiration, comes that ineffable love that glows forth in waves of peace and healing to all mankind. Out of stillness, all is made one.

What urges one to go apart and seek stillness? Is it the holy essence of Spirit that is the soul of man? God calls the man to prayer. Trust in the living purpose of Is-ness. That which creates knows all; therefore, have faith in its wisdom.

Stillness is no more than an opportunity to be more fully aware of the livingness, the energy, the sublime tranquility that is allness.

Listen to the stillness. It holds you and holds all around you. You do not contain, you are contained. All is contained. This power and energy is what you are. You cannot be outside it; outside is an illusion, an error. When all words cease, all effort to encompass ends. This tremendous principle of stillness is the conscious awareness of life. It is the clarity that resurrects man and his world.

Tuning in to the essential is not a thing of human will or design but simply stopping right where one is and being empty of human business and desire. The vacuum is instantly filled with the sweetness, the joy, the tranquility of divine Love—that mysterious energy expressing all life and much more.

□□□□□□□

Listen; hear the soundless voice that sings the wondrous song of love. It is the song that transforms, raises up, and makes whole. Listen deep; listen wide.

□□□□□□□

Meditation is being aware of the presence of infinite Is-ness within.

□□□□□□□

When we seem to have lost the glimpse, we immediately try to think it back. Wrong way! It doesn't come back with any amount of thinking. Forget thinking. Be still, and you'll see you have gone nowhere and have lost nothing.

□□□□□□□

Experience the absolute and fill all needs. All is revealed as you leave the concept of two and experience only one. Dropping and surrendering all familiar terms ends the limitations of the picture that senses provide.

When you are still enough to realize that the Holy One is right here now, then you experience the One as all. Rather than thinking it, it is being it that lets the light of it shine forth.

□□□□□□□

When I am willing to know nothing, be nothing, and simply wait— empty—and listen, then magically I am whole, united.

□□□□□□□

Life

Life is continually unfolding and being its own purpose. As humans, we fight it and try to bend it to our personal wishes, to the way we think it should be. Here is where we meet pain head on. When we can simply let life be itself and remove our attempts to interfere, then harmony reigns and the plan becomes visible as perfection.

Get out of the way of life. Surrender the personal sense of self and clear the way for the unfolding of God's purpose.

Life is continual change. Usually, the longer it seems to remain static, the more noticeable the change when it comes. Look at the nature of all living things. Change is going on day by day. It is up to us to go with change, to be open to it to find what the greater purpose is for our individual experiences.

Life is eternal, but it is born into a time belief that says it is an endurance of only so many days. If you are a counter of days and years, it is not surprising that this counting leaves its signature on your face and body.

The secret of life and true knowledge lies in not thinking, not concepting, just being still and listening, watching, and waiting. Being aware that every breath is given by God, every step is God's, every moment of awareness is God's.

Thinking is the trap in which separate belief is born. Thinking is a sickness from where all sicknesses proceed. The burden of riches and the burden of poverty, the burden of possessions and of wanting or losing or gaining are all aspects of thought. Stillness is nonthinking, nonconcepting. But go further than either thinking or nonthinking. . . .Hush; do not utter a word.

Go with the rhythms of life. Bend like a reed or a willow. After a peak of activity, be ready for the quiet place in preparation for the rise that follows. Never resist. Never grieve after yesterday. Never look for tomorrow. For what is, is here now. Watch in tranquil surety where you are.

Having the courage to let go and stop trying to possess life works miracles. Let go, and you have it all. It is getting out of the way of the natural power of life to live that heals. This is faith that evidences miracles. It is never too late to turn away from the belief in sickness and pain. Realizing that there is nothing in the universe to worry about is the healing frame of mind.

God is all there is. This life you are is not yours; this life is God's. Awareness is not a person's belonging, it is God's awareness. We have nothing, we are nothing but a manifestation of the allness that God is. This continual recognition is the only true life—all else is make believe. We surround ourselves with junk while the gift of infinite worth is right here as what we truly are: the love of God is all we are.

Every moment of the day you are in the presence of God, and every act is holy. It is the difference between living in hell and living in heaven. Every detail of living is Is-ness. You always have the choice of which road to walk. The grace is in the point of view. How you perform every moment and how you recognize omnipresent divinity is what is important, not a judgment of whether the task is a chore or is "good." Every moment is precious. Life is all opportunity to be It and not outside of It.

The happiness that is beyond anything money can buy needs no equipment, no expense—nothing at all that the world can offer. Such priceless contentment and joy is ever at hand. It cannot be acquired; it is already here. It is what you really are underneath all the blindness of personal senses. Here is the perfection of life. It is the gift given to everyone. It is but to be realized and honored.

The feeling of riches is interpreted at a low level as dollars, but the feeling is not limited to the world's view of wealth. Infinite supply is evident as Life in all its countless forms. Potential is ever present as Principle. The infinite wealth of Principle makes earthly riches into nothing.

Man uses Life for his personal desires. He does not see what it is or see the wonder of it. He goes through his life ignorant of where or how he is and never enjoys the real riches of Life. He counts in dollars and years and time and houses and bodies, and he is blind to Life eternal right here. Man honors person, the passing shadow, and misses the glory of Is-ness.

Know the evenness and balance of a life founded upon awareness of God's continual presence. Oh joyous and timeless are the servants of the Christ of God. Knowing this reality, it is a wonder that attention can be diverted to illusionary things to be worried about. Giving of one's wholeness to the Christ of God fills the heart and mind until there is no room for little thoughts, cares, or worries.

How beautifully our eyes are adjusted to the amount of light that this planet receives. How wonderful the breath of air for which we are made. We are made perfectly to live under these conditions. We inhabit a body specialized for these conditions. See it all for the wonder it is. Praise and love the designer, the spirit that guides and makes possible all things. Be still and look beyond human sight.

We are to make the first move in the right direction, and then help comes. Help does not come to those who refuse to take the first step. This first step is reaching away from the belief in separateness to belief in the source of all. When we have reached out in selfless love and recognition, the next step is revealed to us. Each step brings us closer to unity with the source of all, from which all comes and to which all returns.

What is seen as a dazzling galaxy of stars might be only a pale shadow of what is. Therefore, do not judge anything by limited sight. Whether expanded by telescope or microscope, it is still a limited view. Proceed only as the heart evidences the truth to be. Before the scientist pronounces his new theory, the heart has drawn aside the curtain and has revealed Is-ness, for Is-ness is ever known. It is for us to open our hearts and minds to it.

We seem to be locked into beginnings and endings. All our lives, we are geared to starting and ending, being born and then dying. Ills begin and we look for an end. Projects have beginnings and endings. We are ever coming and going. It is a pattern built on the day-and-night qualities of this three-dimensional planet life.

Most of us are caught up in this two-ness and see no way out. We are brain conditioned to beginnings and endings, none of which has anything to do with divine continuity. We must lift our view out of this established pattern of always expecting endings.

Omnipresent activity as conscious awareness does not begin or end. Realizing this would free us of the belief in beginnings and endings. Realizing this would take us out of this limited state and into the boundless state of divine continuity. To be constantly aware of this continuity of reality is bliss. It is wholeness.

Many have the fixed belief that one has to die to reach heaven. I tell you this is not so. Heaven is here right now, and if it is not found and entered now, no amount of dying is going to get you there. Conscious life is it; say, "I exist. I AM." This is the wonder.

Look at any creation and see it free of personal judgment. It is a thing wondrously made of color, form, and adaptability. But it is brief and ever changing, and like a shadow at evening, it is gone.

We cling to our form—why? Are we afraid that this is the only form of our awareness? This belief belittles life and denies the eternal quality of it. Because we are looking at a form of life dependent upon certain planetary conditions, we moan that there is no such life anywhere else. Life adapted to these conditions, and it follows that it adapts to any conditions anywhere. Life, the principle, is universal, eternal. Spirit that is that principle is never without form.

When we come to the end of a road, the habit is to turn about and retrace our steps. Let's try going on where there is no road. Get out of the car and walk that field, that hill, and cross that stream. When you leave the pavement, you realize a new power of enjoyment and the feeling of true freedom lifts you up. Of course, the pavement and the car are our conditioning; the field, hill, and stream are the adventure of discovery in consciousness. It is inner attention that opens our lives to reality.

The heart yearns for its natural home. Here, bound to flesh and all the ills that flesh is heir to, the heart yearns for the freedom and beauty it really is. Listen to the heart of hearts. It sings a song incomparable. Let it not starve, but feed it with attention. Listen to its song. Live the way it tells of and hell is transformed to heaven and all ills are transcended. Listen! Follow! All is here, right here as the awareness and wonder of I AM.

Recognition and awareness, not ministry, changes us. Our greatest ministry is to be the Light so that all can see the truth in themselves and glorify it. In our activities of "good works," we are like fleas on a dinosaur, but by being the perfection we preach about, we are servants of God.

Look not at the sad, distracted world and moan, but see what is right here and now as the glory and wonder that life is. As each of us turns his face inward with Love, the world is new. Only by seeing the Light here at home is the service to man performed.

If you would live, really live, then surrender the belief in a me who owns everything, even a body. Relinquishing this is most difficult because the person idea clings to the concept of itself. But real identity is the identity of God the divine Spirit felt in the deepest caverns of the heart as Love ineffable. Surrender by filling your consciousness with the seeing and understanding of God's constant presence everywhere here and now.

Yesterday, I saw a venerable live oak, its great arms spread forth holding up its canopy of perennial green. This old oak has seen people come and go, generations of change, and its silent mystery stands ever vulnerable, a symbol of life's wonder.

An oak such as this attracts attention by its age and generous shadow on a hot day. Its beauty comes to bloom in age. It is not moved by those who come to be amazed by its mighty trunk and symmetry. It simply is, and it is its being that makes man look upon his own petty ways, hopes, desires, and fears. The oak reveals so much more than what appears as living wood and twig and leaf. It sings a song to the listening one of cause, of energy made from that something beyond all manifestation.

□□□□□□□

The appearance of the aging body belongs to the world of limited beliefs where all appears to be born, to age, and to die. Only spirit is real. Do not be caught in the world of appearance, which is illusion and is passing. Keep your attention fixed only on that which is eternal and infinite. Keep your attention focused on the eternal I AM.

□□□□□□□

Do you feel sometimes that you are at your wit's end? That you are harried and desperate with nowhere to turn? It could be the most positive state in your life. Right where there appears to be a hopeless mess is the grand opportunity to take the next step beyond into seeing and feeling Truth. It is coming to understand that just a step away from wit's end is heaven, Is-ness. If you are truly at your wit's end, you are forced to surrender, to relinquish your hopeless trying and struggling, and to really listen to conscious awareness.

In that listening, desperation turns to wonder, and wonder to amazement, and amazement to seeing that you are not a separate, harried person but an inheritor of the Kingdom of Heaven.

□□□□□□□

Love

Love without desire or attachment is the gift of God. Care for it and nourish it as a treasured child. Love has greater power than any device for violence man can invent. Love gives without hope of return. Its giving is its joy and its nourishment. Love knows no fear, no want, no concern. Love knows no confinement, no bounds, no limits, no legislation. Thanks be to God for love as an aspect of God that penetrates all dimensions of God's universe.

How does one begin the boundless knowing of perfect, unattached love? Where one is right now. The true nature that is the Self knows this infinitude of love. Look beneath the worldly sheath for the Self, the very I you are. Infinite love is already there. But it also is to be revealed in what appears as every individual who crosses your path. When you find it as your Self, you find it everywhere.

Love of infinite proportions sows its seed within the heart and illumines all darkness with its radiant light. How may this wonder be shared with the world? Send it forth in streams of healing force, and let what is steer its unidirectional course. It is like the sun whose rays go forth in darkness and light all with living glory, giving infinite life where none was before. This is the experience of

Love beyond the self. This radiant energy strikes another heart, and it stirs that heart and fills the night with singing sweetness.

□□□□□□□

Love is often twisted into something of our own desire or belief as an attachment of a person for a person. But Love, real Love, is as God: unattached, universal, unselfed, and unobjectified. Until this pure Love is realized, healing is only temporary. True healing is the realization of Love as pure unity of all Spirit. Rise above what the mortal sees and lift the heart to the permanent, divine Spirit.

□□□□□□□

Dynamic love knows no limits or desire or attachment. Stillness is its medium. Silence is its song. Listening is its joy. Being is its fulfillment. Awareness is its Is-ness. It is all we are. Its radiant energy is the light of the universe.

□□□□□□□

Positive action always finds sufficient energy present. It is attracted to use, and it lies dormant when unused. Energy and Love are both terms for infinite qualities. Real Love is not a static state. Love is immediately present, as sharing and as giving. Energy and Love thrive on active use, especially if freed from beliefs in "me" benefits. There never was and never will be a lack of Love and Energy where actively expressed. They are multiplied by outgoing use and diminished by ingoing self-concern.

□□□□□□□

Foster the feeling of Light within you. Let it grow; let it glow. It is the saving grace, the gentle angel, the freeing and healing agent that is Love uncomplicated by desire or object.

□□□□□□□

Understanding without compassion is not understanding. Love that loves some and not all is not love. Love knows no divisions. Love cannot be annotated.

□□□□□□□

Love does not compel nor can it be compelled. Love waits. Love sees. Love knows Love's own.

□□□□□□□

If you love the creator, then you love all that the creator created. You cannot have love here and distaste there for such is borne of judgment. When your eyes are clear of personal desire, you see beauty in all. If you understand, you cannot love a rose and despise a nettle. Love given tirelessly all of itself finds ever more love to give.

□□□□□□□

There is a difference between being empty and feeling empty. To be as an empty glass is being ready to receive. To feel empty is to have the glass turned down and unable to receive.

□□□□□□□

There is nothing so strong in this world as the power of Love— Christ revealed.

□□□□□□□

Energy is boundless and omnipresent when another is in need of help. That boundless energy is God. If the will is present and the need is imperative, one can do the seeming impossible. Love finds a way.

□□□□□□□

Can electric current be seen in its dual state of negative here and positive there? No, it becomes visible light and heat and power only where the two are made one. Likewise, Love separated into beliefs of good and evil is dormant potential. Seeing and understanding makes the two one. Love is. Love like true happiness needs nothing of the world to bring it forth. Love born in one justifies the world.

□□□□□□□

Be the generator of Love's energy and send it forth to all the peoples of the world. Let it shine. Let it flow. It is the essence of Life. Generating divine Love energy fills one to overflowing. It is the bursting forth of the overflow that illumines the Earth.

□□□□□□□

The gift of divine understanding is the gift open to all mankind. It is up to each of us to discover and accept it and make of it a living Light.

□□□□□□□

The secret of Love that changes the world is already in the heart.

□□□□□□□

Forgiveness is a sign that you are closer to the wonder called Love, for no one can come close who harbors a judgment of another in the heart. Through forgiveness, which is Love, you are loosed from the fear, sickness, and anger in the hearts of so many. To know and feel Love ineffable cleanses the heart of all human weakness and lifts you up to God.

A great friend once told me to treat every problem with Love not war, that war only deepens the problem. Make peace with the ego and through Love have it join you and work for you in glorifying God.

All comes forth from focused Love—health, wealth, and tranquility. Love is the wand that enlivens the giver and his works. Nothing of value, of beauty, of worth comes forth without Love for the wonder that Life is and that all of us are.

Truth

Understand this triangle of truth: Stop looking back. Walk out of the shadow. Behold the living Spirit!

Stop looking back. Cease from the belief in time. Time is a convenience of human existence. It is the duality world that is the shadow.

Walk out of the shadow. Get out of the duality beliefs in which most of humanity is suffering from. Discard the belief in separateness from God. When out of that shadow, then this is seen as truth: God is all as all.

Behold the living Spirit. Here is the true home of all individual expression of God. We are all glorious Spirit. We are intangible spirit in the tangible body. Let this truth leap like a flame from heart to heart to light up the world.

When you can understand that you are the truth you seek and that the truth knows no person of conditioned or limited thinking, then you have arrived at human fulfillment. When you know that you are the principle that conscious awareness is, then you are ready to take new steps into enlightenment.

I AM is a universal truth. This is true union. All mankind can know this—not just Christians or just Moslems or just Buddhists or just any group in world-bound separateness. Let the celebration be by and for all mankind so that the spirit that is Love may enter all hearts without regard to color, race, religion, or any other connotation of separate belief.

All I know is that I exist. That is all I can say that is fact. I AM. I AM. I AM. That is all. Everything else added to that is speculative, relative, or derivative. I know I AM. That is all I know. This is truth: I AM. And I AM that truth because I know it. Stripped of all conjecture, wish, or personal dramatization, I know only one reality: I exist. Not "me" but I. I let all else go but this one sure knowing. I AM. I AM. I AM.

Truth is present all around us and as us. We are not the bodies we inhabit. We are the principle reality of conscious awareness in flesh, with the purpose of awakening us to the infinite wonder Being is.

Truth comes to the inner ear in the depth of silence, in utter stillness. The heart knows but hides its secrets from the busy mentality of human affairs. Listen deep beyond thought and you will discover the wondrous beauty of the real that is beyond the unfolding of thought. It is pure experience, pure feeling, beholding of being, the very light that is the principle that consciousness is—so warm, so gentle, so exquisite and yet so strong.

When we let go of the last pretty concept of what we think heaven is, we will be more ready to receive the truth and enter "heaven."

Truth may appear in countless ways, but there is only one truth. It is ever the same no matter what costume it appears in. Truth is ever with you in the center of you. To feel it is bliss, and its enormity can never be encompassed in thought. Only when thought is at rest is the beauty and wonder of truth realized.

There is a too-widespread belief that writings about Truth are only for the unoccupied and not for the busy man or woman. I have heard, "But is it practical? Is the knowing you speak of any use to the average man and woman whose days are too full for sitting in meditation or musing on the infinitude of the universe?"

Well, these questions suggest that enlightenment is something extra and something other than everyday living. Enlightenment is life. If there is no awareness of what life really is, is one really living? Or is one simply acting blindly as in a dream or fumbling about in a lightless room?

As falseness is pared away like an unwanted husk, life becomes more and more of living as praise. Every act, every action is praise. Thought, word, and deed are prayers of praise and loving devotion. It is simply the essential, the continued recognition of that which is all as all. This is joy beyond the knowing of the world at large.

There are truths that never have to be studied but that are always known. It is one of the wonders of life. We know much more than any worldly knowledge that has ever been learned. It has only to be plumbed in stillness.

□□□□□□□

The more we struggle for knowing, the farther away we are. It is up to us to really see that the heart already knows all there is to know because it is eternally here and now. There is nothing else, and the mind of duality is put away and the mind of dual thought is quieted. Put all struggles and wishing aside and know that you already are that which you seek.

□□□□□□□

Wisdom is not necessarily the result of studying terms. Wisdom, if one is truly and openly aware, is as much realized in walking through a garden or along a beach. I have long sought the simple intelligence of the field daisy—pure being without terms—which reflects the glory of the source, God the Father, omnipresent Mind.

□□□□□□□

Spirit

The Living Spirit is omnipresent as light, as vibrating energy, all around us. It is infinite supply and possibility waiting for our recognition and use. What greater gift could be given to mankind than this. Take hold of this power all around us! The impossible is now possible. We are heirs to the Kingdom. Let the Light shine as the intelligence we are so that all may see the wonders of the Father.

The limitation of the human, bound to a three-dimensional idea, can never know Is-ness in the terms of three dimensions. But as Spirit, which is the reality of man, knowledge is present everywhere. As Spirit, one is master over all human belief. Watch for every new realization of an infinite Self. In entering the unknown, take nothing with you that has been told before—nothing! You will be amazed, and there, after amazement, is understanding.

This wonder we call Love that we feel springing up within us without any worldly cause makes living a supreme adventure. It can happen to anyone—young or old. It is not dependent upon age, condition, place, or any event. Like the sun, it simply is, and it changes man from a harried worrier or a horrid warrior to the joyfulness of a little child. It is this love that bursts the skin of conditioning and rises to unwordable heights of consciousness. It is peace, tranquility, joy, and so much more that it can only be called ineffable wonder.

The body is the housing of Spirit and as such is a wonder in itself. The body is a fine servant. As a master, it is a delusion that hides one from one's reality. But trained and controlled, the body is the Spirit's experience in this dimension. It carries us here and there and performs feats or reflects the Light within it. Its purpose is to serve the Spirit not an ego.

Even with abuse and misuse heaped upon the body, including negative and destructive thinking, Principle maintains life. Everything of senses is after the fact. The way to health and wholeness is keeping attention on the wonder that conscious life is. The practice of love fills one with joyousness, and the body responds with Life.

Spirit is the vibrating energies of life. Unless this truth is recognized and practiced, there cannot be wholeness of life. It is odd how we separate healing from the natural wholeness of all that is. Even as we acknowledge that Spirit is all, we more often than not image a particular healing as something separate and is prayed for separately. Wholeness as the natural state of being is the full awareness of Holy Spirit being all, which means nothing is outside or separate. To be whole, we are to be fully aware of the omnipresence of Spirit.

Man is custodian of God's wonder and awareness. As long as one seeks for personal pleasure or betterment, one seeks only illusion and delusion. Seek to know, to feel the presence of Reality. That which resides in the glowing heart is the power that can change, heal, and bring order and tranquility out of chaos.

Our roots are spirit. It is natural that we turn back to them. We are already spiritual beings. We are cased in a body of flesh in this phase, but we are really Spirit. We can never separate ourselves from our roots any more than a tree can walk away and leave its roots.

Nothing stands between us and our salvation and enlightenment but ourselves with our continued preference for dreams rather than reality. Some find the books they read as crutches to lean on. Others lean on a group or a particular leader or teacher. There is always an alternative to going alone into the very core of the emptiness within us. To do so is to discover in amazement that here in that infinite void is nirvana. Here is the source of all energy and the potential of the infinite universe.

I am dancing. I am joy expressed. This is joy without any worldly cause. Whether this appearance is 8 or 80 makes no difference whatever. I am ageless. This one who dances—this self, this invisible reality—is ever here. It makes no difference if the physical appearance is asleep, alive, or dead. I dance. I praise. I enjoy. I am eternal. I am neither male nor female. I am all. I am pure consciousness. I am in perfect equilibrium. I am a whole, beautiful, loving Being. And I am this timelessly, spacelessly. I sing. I dance. I celebrate the glory of Being—almighty Being.

□□□□□□□

Surrender is a moment-by-moment attention to the power that is expressing as conscious life. To have total faith and surrender to Love that functions and cares for you asleep and awake is the happiest and most successful of living.

If keeping attention on this intangible essence of life is tiring, then your attention is not on it. With attention wholly on that which is, there is no fatigue, no ennui, no struggle. There is fulfillment! Loving the wonder that is conscious awareness with your body and your spirit and all your mind and strength is living and loving the divine life!

□□□□□□□

As we move along the way, we discover we really do nothing of ourselves, and the less the better. As we surrender our personal ownership of our lives and let go, give over the reins to Spirit, all is done for us. We are led, we are inspired, we are raised up, we are glorified. As the attention is on God, all things are added unto us. The way is made easy.

□□□□□□□

God forgives, but does man forgive himself? Do not disturb the waters of life with judgment. Let it be. So often we struggle to uphold a well-taught human standard, and in so doing, we disturb the peace of being and imperil the natural tranquility of bliss. Be constantly aware and disturb as little as possible.

□□□□□□□

You might think you are far off because you cannot feel the bliss in your heart, but you are never any farther away. The Presence never varies. It is. Whether you are aware does not change the nearness of the Presence.

Turn on the light to dispel the darkness. If you choose to sit in the darkness and be afraid, there is nothing to be done until you see the error and reach for the light. This is not a struggle to "get back." You were never anywhere but here, and you can never be anywhere but here where Spirit is. You are already in the Kingdom of Heaven.

As winter changes to spring, the daylight begins to linger and we turn back to the light, to the sun. The spirit celebrates again as darkness is overcome. Darkness is only the result of turning from the light. Let us always turn away from shadows and look to Light, for Light is and dark is not.

Each of us has buried deep within an assurance of immortality that we can never prove in present dimensions or with our limited logic and reason. But it is here as the very consciousness awareness we are. It is a subtle, indefinable knowing that we the living principle do not go into perpetual nothingness at death. Our sense of nothingness is purely relative to our belief in a solid-appearing world, but that belief is no good anywhere but as planetized people.

Awake and see! This seeing is not with eyes of flesh, but it is seeing with the heart. And this is not a heart of flesh, but it is the center, the core in the depths of one's being. This understanding frees one from the confines of a persona or mask. This is essential to feel the awareness that is of no sex, color, belief, or human desire.

This is the void that most are afraid to look at. It is the immensity that is as all phenomena, form and no form. It is energy of being, the force within the seed. It is what you really are. It is why you are to see through the mask the world has woven around you. Then you see what does not die, does not fade. It becomes and becomes and returns until perfect as the force that made it grow. It is united as one with the wonder Being is.

Where the world seems to press in on you, that is where you stop feeling like a victim and take command. Be that which you are. Master this appearance world, and do it easily and well. Not as one superior but as one loving all of God's universe. Call Spirit into action. All is possible to you. Never feel subject to anything. You have played the trembling leaf too long. Now see nothing in this world as beyond the power of Spirit.

Full attention on the wonder of Is-ness is joy to your spirit and is wholeness to the body. Do not mistake a feeling of physical well-being for a joy of spirit. Physical well-being can change from one day to the next. The feeling of Love wholly attentive does not alter. If your joy is dependent on any thing, person, or worldly condition, it is not lasting joy. It is not real.

The heart feels the warmth of divine consciousness as the body feels the warmth of the sun.

□□□□□□□

The seed of God is planted in us and awaits the gentle rain of understanding to cause it to grow and flourish. Love is that seed. Glory and wonder are hidden within that seed. Freedom is there; all goodness is there. It always was and it always will be. Let it grow and let it bloom.

□□□□□□□

To be aware of the wonders of God's universe from the smallest and the greatest appearances is to live in a continuous happy state of mind called Heaven.

□□□□□□□

Put your faith where it never finds disappointment or failure: God the source, God the substance, God the only and all.

□□□□□□□

God's universe is here, the same as it was at first conception. It is all light and wonder. You can be it. You can live it as your very real self.

□□□□□□□

Gifts

Treasures, gifts are everywhere. One but takes the time to see them. Once, long ago, I walked along an unused trail among the desert hills. The trail led me to a sheltered cove behind rocky cliffs. This cove, cut off from all view of man, held unseen, except by one alone, a crowded garden of flowers, so thickly growing that I could not move lest I crush them. Yellows, mauves, purples, whites—all sweetening the air with untamed perfume.

Chance? Perhaps. Is it chance that I came upon it and experienced the gift, the joy of it? Perhaps I was drawn there to behold the beauty of the consciousness I AM. Perhaps that far secluded place, that secret place, also had to share its treasure.

Each day is a new mystery, a new wonder that is unweighted by yesterdays or tomorrows. Newness is nowness, with every moment nothing but the presence of almighty Being. Every moment is a celebration and the celebrant is the I aware of I AM.

Never forget those who have given help. So often, when things appear easy and one is full of wholeness, we tend to overlook those who came wholeheartedly to our assistance and gave of themselves and substance to help. Let appreciation remain ever in the heart and be recognized openly.

All help comes through unattached love, through God-ness that leads the way and comforts and stills human cares. The law in operation here is as much a part of our lives as gravity. It is the law of give and receive, receive and give. In return for care, feeding, and watering, the fruit tree gives of its fruit. Understood, the flow of supply is unbroken.

At day's end, there is a special accounting, a recognition, of the true and everlasting Being. All around us are treasures. We walk among riches untold; yet, they are rarely seen, and they are barely understood. We live in radiant energy. We live in vital Spirit, not a world of time and space or any other concept of smallness or largeness. Beyond all opposites is the conscious being I AM.

Talent is a joyous thing. It is not to be pushed or forced or made to do what personal sense has in thought. It is to be itself. Talent is a gift of that Is-ness we are. Guard it; nurture it with care and kindness but never treat it with possession or attachment. Talent belongs to all, not one or two. It thrives on sharing and being shared. See how the magic of talent turns an ordinary event or experience into a wonder, a jewel to be treasured. Talent is recognized by the heart, by Spirit. If it is not appreciated by its channel, then it returns to dormancy and waits. Talent is the smile of God. It is harmony. It blooms in love and in gentleness. Talent is a joy forever. Treasure it.

Solitude has a purpose because—God being all, Mind being all, Awareness being all—nothing occurs without purpose. God's universe is perfect. It is resistance to God's purpose that brings trouble. Struggling against it only makes it more difficult than it need be. Therefore, surrender and the quicker the purpose will be revealed. Honor solitude and make the most of it that you may fulfill God's purpose. End resistance and let the full worth of solitude be revealed. Learn the purpose divine and bless it.

Each dawn is new and unexpected—a gift of life. How is one to justify this gift of life? It is to give to everyone the ineffable, untouchable, unnamable Love. To do this, one is to experience this Love and be a channel through which it flows out like the rays of the sun: in all directions, freely given, freely received.

If one had a great benefactor who continually gave gifts vital to your life, would you go hours—days—attached to something else and give no thought to recognize the giver of such gifts? How can one be so careless of the giver of all gifts, the giver of life and awareness itself? Ineffable love simply gives regardless of reward or recognition.

Simply ask with true desire to be free. Knock at the door of your heart. Seek in your deepest being and you will find freedom in the principle of conscious awareness. The truth so tremendous is all around you, which is the solidity and reality of conscious awareness as God as your Source eternally. If you ask sincerely for awareness of God's eternal presence, it comes to you and changes your life.

You are ever on the threshold of beginning. Being aware of conditioning and separate belief is the constant teacher that is revealing the dead ends you pursue and is showing you the joy of freedom from personal sense.

Through opening the heart to its Light, you grow. Unspeakable joy is in rising up out of the dream and shaking it off and being free of it so that you are again humble, simple, grateful, and loving. Who can stand before the blazing light of purity and not be humbled? How can you not be grateful for each day that turns you from the small to the wonder of whole being?

Let the Light shine upon you. Reach out to it. Embrace it. Be it! It is yours!

Enlightenment cannot be en masse. A plant might cast 10,000 seeds, but only a few take root and grow and flower.

Every day is a holy day. Every moment, every breath are beyond words to write or speak.

Afterword

Once opened, the inner eye remains so. If you are aware of not experiencing Light in your daily living, that is the first step.

Simply continue being aware of not-ness and you will be led into Is-ness. Suddenly, one day, you will see the blindness you have lived.

The Light is then present, and all shadow vanishes. The Light discloses the cause and eliminates it.

David Joseph Manners

Books by William Samuel

A Guide to Awareness and Tranquillity

> *The entire Universe of Truth has been within us all the while—within the Heart! Here! Now!*

Discover a peace of mind and tranquillity that are utterly beyond belief. Discover an unfluctuating, unchanging, permanent sense of well being that transcends every human concept. This volume is intended to prove that awakening to Reality is nearly effortless.

290 pages, ISBN 1-877999-19-9

The Awareness of Self-Discovery

> *This book is for those who want Illumination itself, not a description of it—and for those who want to know how to live it.*

This companion to *A Guide to Awareness and Tranquillity* expands the themes presented in that book. This book is for those who want peace of mind and are prepared for it. Those who are prepared are those who are willing to leave old landmarks—willing to forsake ego and intellectuality. Those who do will find these words instantaneously effective.

200 pages, ISBN 1-877999-04-0

The Child Within Us Lives!

Dedicated to the carefree, joyful, triumphant Child within each of us!

The Child Within Us Lives! brings science, religion and metaphysics alive. Eclectic and non-sectarian, it puts, quantum physics, psychology, philosophy, and metaphysics in a new perspective, beyond theory and speculation. Our real identity, The Child and Its guidance, is essential in our search. The Child of Light and Love is the pathfinder, the guide, the wayshower. Science, religion, and philosophy can take us a great distance, but the Child takes us to Dominion.

400 pages, ISBN 1-877999-09-1

Two Plus Two Equals Reality

There is a simple and gentle Light within these pages that will change your life and make all things new. It can! It will! But it is a message only the Heart can find. Search with the Heart and you will find it.

58 pages, ISBN 1-877999-07-5

William Samuel's books can be ordered through any bookstore in the United States or internationally.

For more information, to order books directly, and to order CD recordings of presentations by William Samuel, call 805-646-8179 or go to www.williamsamuel.com.

To write to William Samuel and Friends, send email to sandy@williamsamuel.com or send letters to Sandy Jones, 307 N. Montgomery St., Ojai, CA 93023.

David Manners was a Broadway actor, star in the Golden Age of Hollywood, best-selling novelist in the 1940s, and a life-long searcher for spiritual truth. From 1978 to 1993, he kept a daily journal, recording his ideas on spirituality, which he called "a conversation between the soul and the Spirit." The posthumous publication of *The Wonder Within You* is his third metaphysical book.

David Morgan Jones, editor and publisher of *The Wonder Within You,* is an editor, writer, and manager in the corporate world by day, and a researcher and biographer by night. He can be reached at this e-mail address: dafyddmj@comcast.net.

Printed in Great Britain
by Amazon

70769697R00113